DIVINELY DESIGNED

How to Surrender to the Potter's Hand,
Go Through the Fires and Crises of Life and Become His Masterpiece

By

Emmanuel Borbon, Aleli Grace Corpuz,
Leni Del Prado, Patrick Del Prado,
Jackie Morey, Mildred Osias, Raymond Osias,
Enrique Sarthou, Agnes Sarthou, Dante Simon and Rolland Wright

DIVINELY DESIGNED

How to Surrender to the Potter's Hand,
Go Through the Fires and Crises of Life and Become His Masterpiece

Published by

Customer Strategy Academy, LLC

16212 Bothell Everett Hwy, Suite F111, Mill Creek, WA 98012

Publisher Jackie Morey's email: CustomerStrategyAcademy@gmail.com

Copyright Use and Public Information

Unless otherwise noted, images have been used according to public information laws.

ISBN: ISBN: 978-1-7332501-2-2 Paperback

Limits of Liability and Disclaimer of Warranty

The authors and publisher shall not be liable for the reader's misuse of this material. This book is for strictly informational and educational purposes.

THE HOLY BIBLE, NEW INTERNATIONAL VERSION®, NIV® Copyright © 1973, 1978, 1984, 2011 by Biblica, Inc.™ Used by permission. All rights reserved worldwide. Scripture quotations taken from the New American Standard Bible® (NASB), Copyright © 1960, 1962, 1963, 1968, 1971, 1972, 1973, 1975, 1977, 1995 by The Lockman Foundation Used by permission. www.Lockman.org | The Holy Bible, English Standard Version® (ESV®) Copyright © 2001 by Crossway, a publishing ministry of Good News Publishers. All rights reserved. | Scriptures marked NLT are taken from the HOLY BIBLE, NEW LIVING TRANSLATION (NLT): Scriptures taken from the HOLY BIBLE, NEW LIVING TRANSLATION, Copyright© 1996, 2004, 2007 by Tyndale House Foundation. Used by permission of Tyndale House Publishers, Inc., Carol Stream, Illinois 60188. All rights reserved. Used by permission. | Scriptures marked CEV are taken from the CONTEMPORARY ENGLISH VERSION (CEV): Scripture taken from the CONTEMPORARY ENGLISH VERSION copyright© 1995 by the American Bible Society. Used by permission. | Unless otherwise indicated, all Scripture quotations are taken from THE MESSAGE, copyright © 1993, 2002, 2018 by Eugene H. Peterson. Used by permission of NavPress. All rights reserved. Represented by Tyndale House Publishers, a Division of Tyndale House Ministries. | Scripture taken from the Tree of Life version (c) 2015

Disclaimer

DEDICATION AND ACKNOWLEDGEMENTS

Emmanuel Borbon – To my wife Gem, my son Jon, and my daughter Jen. In this journey your love is unflinching. Thank you for cherishing tomorrow's photograph, for not walking in circles and for pausing when love beckons.

Aleli Grace Corpuz – Dedicated to my Lord and Savior Jesus who rescued me and granted me a brand new EXTRAORDINARY life; and to my husband Roger, and children Richard and Abigail who supported me in this journey.

Leni Del Prado – I dedicate this book to my husband Patrick, my sons Timothy and Silas, my sister in law Nikki, my sisters and brothers in Christ whose stories have become an inspiration, source of joy and strength to me in writing compelling devotions. To my Lord Jesus Christ whom I give the highest honor and praise, without those pathways He so divinely designed, the lessons and wisdom that come from them, my life story wouldn't be half as interesting.

Patrick Del Prado – To my wife Leni, and sons Timothy and Silas, for being my source of joy and inspiration in life.

Jackie Morey – To Abba the One Who divinely designed me and my life, to my Lord Jesus Christ my Redeemer and Conquering King, to the Holy Spirit, to my exceptional Husband Jim, our children Michael and Alyssa, my extended family, and all my friends near and far.

Mildred Osias – To the voices that steered my pen – GOD, Papa Solomon and my late Mama Virginia, Mommy Flor, Raymond, Abdiel, Andrew, Adrianne, Julie, kith and kin whom I love, FCC family especially Denmark, and people who colored my path. Forever grateful.

Raymond Osias – I would like to dedicate this book to my wife Mildred, Abdiel, Andrew, Julie, Tatay Felix, to my late Nanay Rose who was the happiest and proudest person I know when I became a pastor and to my FCC Family in Copenhagen.

Enrique Sarthou & Agnes Sarthou – To our Lord and Savior Jesus Christ who is worthy of all our praise – We dedicate our plans, goals and broken selves … all for your honor and glory alone!

Dante Simon – I humbly dedicate this to the Lord Jesus Christ for all His sustaining love and

provisions. I also offer these with thanks to my wife Vivelyn and our three wonderful boys – David, Stevo and Dante Jr.. Also dedicate this to my family-my father, mother, Tita Ginny, my siblings Jojo, Elzar, Christine, Mark, Jay and Jan. Also in remembrance of Kuya Edgar and baby Ronald (deceased). To God be the glory.

Rolland Wright – "Now to the King eternal, immortal, invisible, the only God, Be honor and glory forever and ever. Amen." 1 Timothy 1:17 TLV

TABLE OF CONTENTS

FOREWORD

"Nothing happens unless you dream."
~Carl Sandburg, American poet

Almost twenty years ago God placed in my heart to be part of a book.

I had little knowledge of how to do it. I shared this with my clergy colleagues, but everyone seemed to be so busy with ministry and raising their young families.

The idea was this: Put together God-fearing, God-loving people who are practicing ministry in a variety of ways in the communities where they serve. The book would be a collection of their sermons, messages, and meditations that would benefit believers and fellow workers who need inspiration, enlightenment, teaching resources, and encouragement.

I waited but nothing happened. Yet the dream didn't die. I held on to the promise because He who started a good work will fulfill it (based on Philippians 1:6).

I waited some more. Still nothing happened.

Then the God of surprises made His move. He reconnected me with my high school classmate, International Bestselling Author and Publisher – Jackie Lansangan-Morey. Similarly, she had a passion to publish something like this.

Our other high school classmates Leni Del Prado and Aleli Grace Corpuz – were excited and also wanted to be part of this project! And with the help of family and friends, another saying kept ringing in my ear written by Cardinal Suenens: *"Blessed are those who dream and are willing to work to make their dreams come true."*

God has willed that the appointed time was almost twenty years later. He assembled these wonderful Christian practitioners and writers to offer this beautiful book "Divinely Designed", title of which is Jackie's idea.

Thank you, fellow collaborators for making this dream come true. Thank You, Lord for planting the dream. Special thanks to Jackie for making this a reality. We humbly offer this book to the Glory of God and the edification of the Saints. Amen.

The Rev. Dante "Bong" Simon
The United Methodist Church, USA
Chaplain, Promedica Heartland, CPSP, Spiritual Care Association USA

CHAPTER 1

CREATED FOR INTIMACY

By
Noel Borbon

A PHOTOGRAPH OF TOMORROW

Tomorrow – another word for **future**.

It was in the decade of my thirties that I was at the summit of Le Moléson, Switzerland.

I stood where earth greeted the firmament, with its assembly of the Swiss Prealps bathed in sun-kissed flushes of summer hues.

In the pinnacle of my photography obsession, I could not resist but preserve the moment in a photograph that would traverse the seasons.

With my DSLR camera mounted on a tripod, I dashed into the frame with the magnificence of creation stretched behind me. Three, two, one... and the percussive sound of the shutter commanded my excitement.

Hoping for a grandiose result, I dashed even faster to view what was captured, but to my bewilderment, instead of suspending time, I travelled it!

It was as if I had travelled 40 years ahead to be exact.

My shrinking posture, weatherworn face and hair, the smoky combination of salt and pepper couldn't argue against this.

When did the sun's warm embrace turn into a bone chilling draft beneath my musty jacket? Where was the dashing young man in distressed jeans and white sneakers?

Of course, that was all just a figment of my vibrant imagination. But I wondered… "Is it possible to take a photograph of tomorrow?"

Could we take a blank canvas and start to paint an impression of a moment years ahead?

Not what it *could* be like, but what it **will** be like.

As if the brush, held by our hand, was mysteriously guided when it hit the grain of the canvas and after all was done – voilà – we stand dumbfounded trying to comprehend what we behold before our eyes.

When my grown-up son was just a little kid and asked what he wanted to become in the future he would always say with a smile, "I want to be a pastor."

Being a pastor myself, this was music to my ears.

Of course, I was fully aware of the challenges of the calling while simultaneously familiar of the indescribable delight that comes when one surrenders to God's beckoning.

My son is now a business analyst. As to how the aspiration to be a pastor vanished…it's a mystery.

Maybe I captured the wrong photograph and he took the right one.

Needless to say, the future is still unfolding. How God would carve the life prepared in advance for my son will surely hint of heavenly sketches.

Come and open the photo box – that is the Bible – and gaze at the 'photographs of tomorrow' that will take your breath away.

The First Set of Photographs - Divine Conspiracy - Jeremiah

> *"Before I formed you in the womb I knew you, and before you were born I consecrated you; I have appointed you a prophet to the nations."* Jeremiah 1:5 NASB

Certainly, this is a photograph that would knock you off of your chair.

What?

Is he talking about a fetus?

But no. This is prior to the prophet being formed in the womb. Before Jeremiah was even conceived in his mother's womb, he was known.

Is this a suggestion that we first existed in the mind of God?

A divine conspiracy indeed!

The apostle Paul confirms this fact in Galatians 1:15a, *"But when God, who set me apart from my mother's womb and called me by his grace."*

God exercised the same thing with Paul and the apostle was wise enough to discern this.

Notice the verbs concerning God and Jeremiah: *"formed"*, *"knew"*, *"consecrated"* and *"appointed."* This sets the plot for Jeremiah's life. The key is for the prophet to recognize God's design and for him to step into that mold.

For me the word *"form"* speaks about shape. Shape is a feature that reveals the uniqueness of a thing.

God has created us unique from each other and this is very special. It gives us significance. It tells us that we are valued and priceless.

The action *"knew"* conveys intimacy. Intimacy is the prelude to continuity.

Observe God's love expressed in Jeremiah 31:3 concerning Israel –

"The LORD appeared to us in the past, saying: 'I have loved you with an everlasting love; I have drawn you with unfailing kindness.'"

God was assuring His people that He would turn their mourning into joy.

This is the part that is constant – God's love – but the continuity of the relationship depends on the love being accepted by the people of God. This entails acknowledging their allegiance, loyalty and faithfulness to him.

Another word for "***consecrated***" is to be set apart.

In some sense it means – *"not meant to be used for anything else"* – exclusive. This, I think, is a sacred privilege. The word clarifies ownership and purpose. The anointing of oil is a beautiful portrayal of this solemn act.

The "***appointment***" settles our mission. Jeremiah was appointed prophet to the nations.

What were you appointed to? This is a lifelong search. Do what you sense the Spirit of God is calling you to. And at times when the path may be dim, when we know He holds us in His hand, we can trust to keep going. God is eager to reveal Himself to us. Be on guard, for He will surely show up.

To be *appointed* is to be a blessing to others. Jeremiah was to be a blessing to the nations.

You can only bless what you can touch. We can never reach everyone, so be mindful of the ones God brings into our circle. However annoying they may be, you were meant to bless them.

Oh, that we may continue to seek His face in unbroken intercourse and learn from Him that we may know His good, acceptable and perfect will.

The future is in God's mind.

The Second Set of Photographs - Daily Cultivation - Joseph

Joseph's photographs were given in dreams. This is how it started – in Genesis 37:5 it says, "Joseph had a dream…"

Do you know that we cannot know God's will unless he reveals it to us? God started to reveal his will to Joseph. Joseph was so excited he told his brothers, and this is how he got in trouble.

We don't have to tell everyone the things God has told us – at least not immediately. It might actually get us in trouble.

Joseph was hated by his brothers because he was special to his father Jacob. In fact, his dad gave him a coat of many colors. And when he told his brothers of his dream, they hated him more.

How sad because even his father rebuked him when told of the dream but at least kept the matter in mind.

He became known as "Joseph the dreamer." Joseph believed in God, but he needed to understand what the dream meant.

The vision matured in Joseph's heart and mind. God was brewing something! It was just a matter of waiting.

I wonder if there are things we have missed in life simply because we were impatient.

…Abraham waited for the birth of Isaac.

…Moses didn't lead the exodus until he was eighty.

…Elijah waited beside the brook.

…Noah waited 120 years for rain.

…Paul was hidden away for 5 years in Arabia.

God was preparing Joseph for a very important *scene*.

In all the preparation there will be seasons of testing, seasons of favor and seasons of silence. Let us hang in there…God is setting the stage.

Joseph eventually ended up in Egypt. There he found favor with the captain of the guard and God prospered him. He did get in trouble again for allegedly raping the wife of the captain and for that went to prison.

Again, he had his moment with dreams – not his, but of the cupbearer and baker who were with him in prison. He interpreted their dreams and they came to pass.

He remained in prison until the cupbearer remembered him as the interpreter of dreams. Through the cupbearer Joseph received an invitation to interpret Pharaoh's dream.

Here's the incredible and important *scene*. Joseph astounded everyone especially Pharaoh by interpreting the latter's two dreams! And to demonstrate his superior wisdom which was from the Lord, Joseph lined out a strategic plan on how to administer the harvests during the first seven years of abundance and plenty, in preparation for the following seven years of devastating famine.

As a result, Pharaoh made Joseph second in command over all of Egypt! Imagine this, Joseph found favor and in one meeting with Pharaoh, was immediately elevated from the dungeon to the palace.

He ended up bestowing such a great contribution to the land and its people, through his incontestable wisdom, exceptional leadership, and extraordinary administration. He was also able to reconcile his family back to himself.

Joseph's secret, I think, was a daily cultivation of his relationship with God. He was a model of personal righteousness. The account in Genesis doesn't reveal his deep conversations with God. The only hint we have is this verse "The Lord was with Joseph." Genesis 39:2 NKJV

The future is revealed in the path of preparation.

Third Set of Photographs – Demonstrated Covenant – Moses

These are photographs that are not easy to look at.

The life of Moses was filled with heartache and pain – heartaches mostly, from the people he served and led towards the Promised Land.

These were hard-headed and stubborn people.

Moses's problems included rebellion, siblings who went contrary to him, the threat from Egypt, harsh conditions, disputes, complaints, lack of food, water and many others.

Aha! Wait a moment. If we read his account, we find a ray of light at the end – towards his death.

Let's first have a look at some details.

Moses lived a total of 120 years divided into 3 periods of 40 years each: 1) starting as prince in Egypt; then 2) shepherd in Midian; and lastly 3) as the leader of the exodus.

The key learning in the life of Moses, and the Israelites he led, is that **"GOD IS FAITHFUL."**

All over the narrative this is proclaimed.

During the many times the Israelites were unfaithful to God, He remained faithful to them.

Paul reinforces this idea in his second letter to Timothy chapter 2 verse 13 – *"if we are faithless, he remains faithful, for he cannot disown himself."*

Moses holds a privileged title of being known as "God's Faithful Servant."

In the book of Numbers, God Himself says that His servant Moses is faithful.

Moses's love was so deep he even asked God to blot his name out of the book God had written if God would not forgive the sin of the people. What a commitment!

There are many dramatic scenes in the life of Moses such as: the burning bush experience, the ten plagues, the Passover, the passage through the Red Sea, the Sinai conversations, the establishment of the covenant, the Ten Commandments, the tabernacle and more.

Through Moses, God established His covenant with his people. This is known as the Mosaic Covenant – named after Moses.

In the generations that came after Moses, throughout history up until the present, God remains faithful. With Jesus as our Mediator, a New Covenant has been established and we are the people of that covenant.

The future is secure for God is faithful to His people and his covenant.

My Photograph

The photograph that has pierced my heart was that of Moses on top of Pisgah when the Lord said to him, *"This is the land I promised on oath to Abraham, Isaac and Jacob when I said, 'I will give it to your descendants.' I have let you see it with your eyes, but you will not cross over into it."*

I cried, and cried, and cried when I read this.

Imagine, this faithful servant of God was not allowed to enter the Promised Land!

My heart was torn.

I was only comforted when I continued reading: *"And Moses the servant of the LORD died there in Moab, as the LORD had said. He buried him in Moab, in the valley opposite Beth Peor, but to this day no one knows where his grave is. Moses was a hundred and twenty years old when he died, yet his eyes were not weak nor his strength gone."*

How affectionate and endearing it was that God would bury the body of Moses.

What these verses tell me is that the Promised Land was not where God finally intended to take him. God took Moses to Himself. The promise to Moses was not a piece of land but a Person.

David captured this beautifully in Psalm 73:26 – "My flesh and my heart may fail, but God is the strength of my heart and my portion forever." In essence when he mentioned "my portion forever," he was saying "God is my inheritance, my future."

Could I take a photograph of tomorrow?

The only way I can do it is not to look at the future as a point in time but to look at it as a Person.

I was indeed at that gorgeous mountain in Gruyères, Switzerland in 2001 taking as many photos as I could. The sights and sounds were gorgeous but didn't make the moment special.

It was a conversation with my Creator that did. For certain, I took a photograph of tomorrow!

WALKING IN CIRCLES

Therefore we also, since we are surrounded by so great a cloud of witnesses, let us lay aside every weight, and the sin which so easily ensnares us, and let us run with endurance the race that is set before us, looking unto Jesus, the author and finisher of our faith, who for the joy that was set before Him endured the cross, despising the shame, and has sat down at the right hand of the throne of God. Hebrews 12-1-2 (NKJV)

A dry and weary land where there's no water

Imagine trudging days on end, aimlessly in a landscape lifeless and parched.

Ahead, a sea of shifting sands parade before your gaze. You turn to look back – at yet another sandy place.

You view right and the scape is unchanged. You veer left, the scene seems unending.

You bend down to look…sand – there is no escape.

And if the dizzying expanse of desert is not already unhinging, you look up and the sunlight is overbearing. Can you ever find your way out of the desert when North looks like South and East looks like West?

In an environment such as this, they say that without visible indicators to guide navigation, people are bound to walk in circles.

One would think that you could consistently walk straight and eventually escape the sandy prison, but unguided strides simply bring you back to where you first started. Some suggest the uneven proportion in leg length is what distorts our bearings even though the difference is subtle.

Others theorize it is because of a variance in leg strength, or perhaps the presence of a dominant leg.

Whatever the reason, when there are no visible markers to calibrate our bearings, it would be close to impossible to leave the wasteland.

Is it the case too, that we walk in circles on a spiritual plane?

Could it be that the fallen nature in humans have brought about a dysfunction in our sense of direction towards God?

Are we, in the spiritual sense, also walking in circles in regard to our relationship with God?

Have we developed a bias that leads us to walk away from the path that He has shown?

Granted this is the case, will the moment by moment practice of His presence take us on a course that eventually eliminates the symptoms of this impairment?

The history of the Israelites is evidence of the condition above. Theirs is a cyclical pattern of behavior and events as follows:

- Pledge of allegiance and faithfulness to God
- Blessing and prosperity experienced
- Complacency eventually leading to unfaithfulness and idolatry
- God sends a messenger
- God's voice is heeded - repentance and renewal follow
- The cycle restarts

This is the history that sets the backdrop of the letter to the Hebrews.

They were currently in a season of persecution. It hadn't escalated yet to executions and death, but their properties were being confiscated and some were taken to prison.

They, too, had their share of *"the desert"* experience. Those who found this unbearable chose to abandon the faith.

With this burden at hand, the writer of Hebrews helps by taking them on this journey in the past and leading them to what God has now done in the present.

Chapter 12 is the pivot point where the writer drops the invitation to this journey of faith.

Let Jesus capture your eyes

"looking unto Jesus…"

He starts with "Therefore," summarizing the exhortation in the previous chapters, then draws them to Jesus.

With an audience possessing a thorough knowledge of Old Testament scripture, the writer capitalizes on this and highlights the supremacy of Christ using contrasts such as that of the sacrifices, and the covenant with Jesus being the perfect sacrifice.

He did this elegantly on several occasions. Thus when he arrives at chapter 12, the words *"Therefore…looking unto Jesus"* becomes so potent to the recipients of the letter.

We can look to Jesus because He is supreme over all. There indeed exists a path to be followed – a way to go…a path headed towards Jesus.

Jesus declared this plainly when he answered Thomas' question *"Lord, we don't know where you are going, so how can we know the way?"* Jesus said, *"I am the way the truth and the life No one comes to the father except through me."* John 14:5-6 NIV

Our faith journey begins by fixing our eyes on Jesus.

Let Jesus write your story

"looking unto Jesus, the author…"

The writer further exhorts them - not just looking unto Jesus but letting Him be the author of this faith journey. The writer did a brilliant recap of their history, so he could tell them this.

Peter reinforces this authorship when he said in Acts 3:15 NIV, "*You killed the author of life, but God raised him from the dead. We are witnesses of this.*"

God is the Author of life and he has a purpose and a plan for His people.

Believe Him and let faith see you through. It is by our will that we believe in God. It is by faith that we are made able to see what we cannot see and once we see, we give ourselves the opportunity to be transformed into His image.

It takes a miracle to become who He has called us to be. We can't even imagine it, but we can prepare our mind, heart and soul to receive His doing, so that the transformation envisioned is accomplished in our being. "*For in him we live and move and have our being.*" Acts 17:28 NIV

To let the Author of life do the writing, is to pursue intimacy with Him.

Faith is the gift that is received in the pursuit of this intimacy. Faith, of course, is not opposed to reason, but faith goes beyond reason. Where reason is unable to explain, faith is the only bridge that can make the connection possible.

Now we know we each have a part in this grand scheme; it is to stick with the plan and let God do the writing of our stories.

Let Jesus finish what he started

"looking unto Jesus, the author and finisher of our faith…"

Now the writer seals the invitation – "looking unto Jesus, the author and finisher of our faith."

At this point you'd expect it to be a done deal with the people whom the writer is reaching out to.

Of course, he goes on to write more on this chapter, and even write another chapter on practical things, but this is the clincher. It's a *"This is it – no turning back – to the death"* moment.

It took the Israelites 40 long years of wandering in the wilderness before reaching the Promised Land when it should only have taken 11 days. Well, they did end up in the Promised Land but what a contrast.

Their plight, in some sense, gives us the impression that they wanted to take matters into their own hands instead of trusting God to complete the journey and fulfill His promise. Whenever they felt things were not going as they selfishly expected, it became a discomfort, and they hailed to go back to Egypt.

Did they lose their appetite for God's presence that they were willing to trade what was promised? Had slavery in Egypt become more glamorous than what lay beyond the Jordan River? Little did they know that one of their future kings will sing a line saying, "Taste and see that the Lord is good; blessed is the one who takes refuge in him."

If we are to trust the Author of life to complete our faith journey, then we have to keep communing with Him.

Spiritual disciplines are venues to center communion with God.

There are several to mention but I just note here the ones I find powerfully engaging: **sacrifice**, **solitude** and **silence**.

Eugene Peterson offers this insight on sacrifice – "*Sacrifice isn't something we do for God but simply setting out the stuff of life for Him to do something with.*"

Fasting is one humbling act of **sacrifice**. It is the practice of self-denial. Many characters in the bible recognize the importance of this discipline. Even Jesus Himself fasted.

We would think that we are at our weakest point when we fast, but actually we are at our strongest point. Fasting is the nourishing of our souls where we develop a deeper hunger for God.

Fasting is not a matter of spiritual technique…it is a matter of our hearts longing to be fed by God.

Solitude is another discipline where we set a space for ourselves away from all the usual distractions of life. It is not an easy place to be.

Here, sensitivity to our fears and the sense of aloneness is heightened. We could feel our insecurities with intensity and the hidden things in our lives are laid explicitly bare.

In solitude, the presence of 'the God who is near' is also heightened. We get to perceive His company and His comfort more sharply. Solitude provides the opportunity to hear Him say *"Fear not for I am with you. I am you refuge. I am your strength. I am your comfort."*

Silence is one I find sacred.

It is total abandon to the One in whom we owe our existence. Our world today has made us accustomed to noise. It is easy to notice this when you're in public transport, that even though no one is talking, half of the crowd has their headphones on. In exercising silence, we deny ourselves of the stimuli noise brings. The holding of our tongue teaches us to speak only when necessary, and when we need to speak, to speak only of the truth in love.

Silence often goes in tandem with **solitude**.

This makes the combination a very effective setting for spiritual transformation.

Note that practicing the above disciplines are not meant to be a therapy session. Approach them with caution.

We surrender to God's presence in these venues of intimacy and allow Him to complete His work in us.

Sensitive to his Spirit

When volunteers were blindfolded, researchers found that a slight deviation in the walk sent information to the brain and thus adjustments were made, resulting in the volunteer-walker tending to walk in a tighter circle.

In the absence of visual markers to calibrate navigation, the brain will use anything available such as sound, texture, smell or taste.

God has provided a lot of signposts and markers to guide us in our faith journey – people, places, circumstances, etc. He even turns our trials into opportunities to transform us. We fix our eyes on Him as He authors and completes our faith journey.

I do not wish to walk in circles; rather I'm heading towards Jesus!

SHE STOPPED IN THE MIDDLE OF A RACE

Thinking about love, I am reminded of a time when my daughter used to be an avid long-distance runner.

She competed in her school's Cross-Country Competition and had consistently represented her school in the district race.

In 2007 she placed 2nd in her school and finished 9th in the district. Unfortunately, it was only the top eight that qualified for regionals.

So, the following year she shortened her running time, placed 1st in her school, and thus competed in the district event one last time.

Based on the trajectory of her performance I was incredibly positive she would do well and secure a spot in regionals.

As I continued to glance at the time, I was so eager to call her and celebrate alongside her. Then the appointed time came. I dialed the number, and without any emotional cues, she answered the phone.

"Hello."

"How was the competition?" I eagerly asked.

"Dad…I placed 60th," she sullenly replied.

I frantically tried to hide my disappointment and allowed a multitude of misfortunate scenarios swarm my thoughts. I was almost convinced she was just pulling my leg.

I gathered myself and allowed my words to formulate, "What happened?"

And this is what she said, "I saw my schoolmate vomiting to the side, so I stopped to help her. When I saw that she was okay, I continued running. Moments after, I saw another friend struggling, and so I paused to help her."

At this moment I could have easily told my daughter that she could have ignored her friends as someone would eventually attend to the situation.

But before I could interject, she added, "*Dad, it is more important to help your peers than to win the race.*"

I sat speechless in my chair. Deep inside, my heart was filling-up with overwhelming joy and I was on the verge of tears.

Thomas Aquinas wrote, "*To love is to will the good of the other.*"

Is this what love really means?

Does it include giving up my dreams? Am I to sacrifice the time, the benefits or the pleasures I deserve? What if the price to pay amounts to forfeiting my life? I certainly have fallen short on many occasions.

O how blessed we are indeed in knowing there is One who loves us with an everlasting love.

The bible describes God's love so wonderfully in John 3:16 NKJV – "*For God so loved the world that He gave His only begotten Son, that whoever believes in Him should not perish but have everlasting life.*"

This verse is one of the most commonly quoted verses in scripture. It summarizes the great drama of love – its **inception**, the **manner** by which it was expressed and the **effect** upon those who willingly will receive.

Inception

"For God so loved the world"

God is the greatest person who has loved. His Triune nature is an endless expression of love.

Can you imagine being loved by the greatest person?

This is so overwhelming, I can't help but pause and cry out, "Thank you, Lord for loving me."

Note that the writer of the gospel of John was commonly known as the "disciple whom Jesus loved." What a privilege to be called as such.

God made love possible to exist in this world by giving us the freedom to choose. He Himself has chosen to love us. He created us in His image and *consistently* wills our good.

The late Ravi Zacharias said that, *"Love is the craving of the human heart to belong in the sacredness of trust and a relationship, and that is what you long for and I long for. God in giving us freedom gave us the greatest possible gift we could ever have with the greatest possible vulnerability at the same time."*

We are incapable of loving, had God not given us the freedom to choose. God initiated the loving. It is up to us to choose to love him in return.

God's love was given to the greatest multitude of people – the world. Indeed the most inclusive – every single soul in the past, present and future – from every race, tongue, tribe and nation.

Whenever tasked to write or speak about love, I always tremble.

Love is so powerful it always grips your being. It is the mystery hidden in the rich textures of feelings, images, sound and color. Visible or invisible; it possesses your soul. Expressed or hinted it arouses curiosity.

Since God is the source of love, the Christian life, if it were not a love affair, can't survive.

The greatest person loved the greatest multitude of people.

Manner

"that He gave His only begotten Son"

Love is the fundamental value of the Christian faith. Any other value in the moral plane is a derivative of love.

The bible emphatically proclaims that God is love. If love is a person, it is quite interesting when we rephrase the above – "Love gave His love."

Could love be expressed any better than in giving your very own and your very best?

In Jesus dwells the fullness of God. God gave Himself to restore the broken relationship between Him, the Creator and us, the created.

The manner by which he has done this is through the sacrifice of Jesus.

Paul in writing to the Ephesians said, "*Follow God's example, therefore, as dearly loved children and walk in the way of love, just as Christ loved us and gave himself up for us as a fragrant offering and sacrifice to God.*" Ephesians 5:1-2 NIV

Talking about giving oneself fully, I can't help but mention the marriage vow:

> "*I … take thee… to be my… to have and to hold, from this day forward, for better, for worse, for richer, for poorer, in sickness and in health, to love and to cherish, till death do us part, according to God's holy ordinance; and thereto I pledge myself to you.*"

Marriage is a lifelong act of giving. To do otherwise is to breach the vow.

The bible speaks of a parallel to marriage with Christ as the bridegroom and the church as the bride.

There is something so potent about giving that makes it hallowed when expressed as a sacrifice. The image we see here is Jesus crucified at Calvary.

It has been said that "You can give without loving but you can never love without giving."

According to Cyril of Alexandria, "*What gives value to a sacrifice is not the renouncement it demands but the degree of love which inspires the renouncement.*"

God expressed his love by giving his only begotten son.

Effect

"that whoever believes in Him should not perish but have everlasting life"

"Whoever" – that sounds outrageous – almost scandalous!

Shouldn't there be any qualifications such as tall, dark and handsome?

Amazing grace indeed – God has made his love available to whoever believes in Him.

To believe in Him is to love Him only.

Deuteronomy 6:4-5 says, "*Hear, O Israel: The Lord our God, the Lord is one. Love the Lord your God with all your heart and with all your soul and with all your strength.*" (NIV). We find Jesus quoting this commandment in the New Testament.

To *not* love God means to love another.

To be frank and brutal, the Bible has a word for that – idolatry.

This was the journey of the Hebrew nation. At one point they would profess their allegiance to God. Then when faced with either abundance or lack, they turned to worshipping idols.

This cycle continued for generations until the New Testament, throughout history and even today.

If we are not mindful of our hearts this could also be our journey.

The promise in the verse is to not perish but have everlasting life.

John 10:10 says, *"The thief comes only to steal and kill and destroy; I have come that they may have life, and have it to the full."* (NIV)

This is the life God promised. Not just a life that is to be expected in the future but one that is available *now.*

I like John Ortberg's take on salvation and our walk with Jesus. The title of his book is, "Eternity Is Now in Session." He conveys that we can start our walk with God now. When we enter into a relationship with God, *eternity begins immediately.*

The psalmist sang *"You make known to me the path of life; you will fill me with joy in your presence, with eternal pleasures at your right hand."* Psalm 16:11 NIV

There is no denying – when love touches you, it changes you.

Once love is given there is no turning back. The lover then lays in wait. The loved will tell us how the story continues. Will love be accepted? Will it be rejected or will there be indifference?

Once in a while, when I come across John 3:16, I read it this way – For God so loved me that He gave His only begotten Son, that since I believed in Him I am no longer going to perish; rather, I am living *now* the everlasting life.

To will the good of the other

It is so easy for our hearts to be maneuvered in another direction. The world could be so seductive and we simply give in with ease.

Who will rescue our hearts?

God is our refuge and strength a very present help in time of need. He is the rudder that steers our souls back to him.

"Dad, it is more important to help your peers than to win the race." – What was my daughter thinking when she said that?

What would it take to stop a person on track toward achieving something that would bring honor, prestige, happiness, merit, respect, admiration or praise?

I'd like to think the answer is **love**.

I will never forget that day when my daughter stopped to help her friends. She came back home without a medal on her neck but I saw two huge gold ones on her heart.

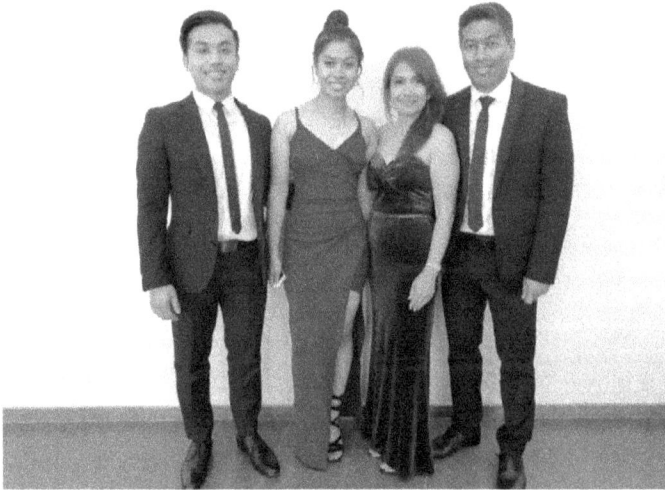

Left to right: Noel's son Jonathan,
Noel's daughter Jennifer, Noel's wife Gemma, and Noel

EMMANUEL "NOEL" BORBON

Emmanuel Borbon is associate pastor of West Sydney Community Church. Prior to this he served in the same capacity at the Love of Jesus Christian Ministries where he was ordained to the ministry.

He is bi-vocational, and having completed a degree in engineering, has been working in Information Technology for around 28 years.

He lives with his family in Sydney, Australia. Originally from the Philippines, it is there he first served in leadership roles at the Power of God Fellowship. He and wife Gemma are blessed with two grown children –Jonathan and Jennifer.

CHAPTER 2

DIVINELY DESIGNED TO BE EXTRAORDINARY

How to live a life of power and purpose

By
Aleli Grace Angeles-Corpuz

Great cities once bustling, glorious monuments of men, spectacular landmarks and grand entertainment arenas humbled to eerie silence remind us that the world has changed.

This is the year 2020 in the middle of the Coronavirus pandemic.

As I write this chapter book in Australia, we are still in lockdown, as are many countries in the world. Every facet of our lives has been affected. All would agree that these recent events have been extraordinary.

But beyond such stark, significant changes in our daily lives, we can sense a much deeper and grander transformation that is also taking place, beyond that which we can see. I do not think I am alone in these musings within my soul.

For many, and not just for believers, the current unprecedented events have resulted in an awakening, a sense of urgency and watchfulness.

For the faithful who trust and long for the Lord's appearing, the call to be ready seems louder and more relevant now than ever before.

We hearken to the words of Jesus in Matthew 25,

> *"1 At that time the kingdom of heaven will be like ten virgins who took their lamps and went out to meet the bridegroom. 2 Five of them were foolish and five were wise. 3 The foolish ones took their lamps but did not take any oil with them. 4 The wise ones, however, took oil in jars along with their lamps....13 Therefore keep watch, because you do not know the day or the hour.'"*

Extraordinary times call for an extraordinary response and demand us to also step into the realm of the extraordinary in the spiritual, to rise up with exemplar faith. We can not live our lives in hopeless defeat as circumstances may incite, but to live a life of power and purpose.

So, I focus on three areas of spiritual instruction in this chapter that I pray will make us steadfast during these challenging times and cause us to live the EXTRAORDINARY lives that we have been divinely designed for.

The first part is about **developing an amazing faith**.

What's *that?*

The type of faith that amazes God. Much has been written about saving faith and perhaps, faith that pleases God. These are foundational.

But I want to talk about the exceptional and write about having an *amazing faith*.

The second lesson is about **prayer** as it relates to our **purpose**.

I think purposelessness is so pervasive in our society. The consequence is that lives have no meaning, pushing people to pits of despair and hopelessness.

I find that even believers are not immune and can lose direction when they embrace a purpose that is not what God intended.

I offer four insights into how prayer is key to establishing our purpose. Now is *not* the time to lose our course!

The last message is rightly placed at the end. It is about **standing firm for the long haul**. In this generation that is marked by a lack of resolve and perseverance, I offer the reminder to finish and finish well.

My prayer is that these words will gird you with strength and make you beautiful till the day of our Lord's return.

Is your faith amazing?
Develop a faith that amazes God

> *'...the centurion sent friends to say to Him: "Lord, don't trouble yourself, for I do not deserve to have you come under my roof....But say the word, and my servant will be healed. ... When Jesus heard this, He was amazed at him, and turning to the crowd following Him, He said, "I tell you, I have not found such great faith even in Israel."'* Luke 7:6-9

There are not too many instances in the scripture when Jesus was amazed at someone's faith.

All too often, faith is *mediocre*, even among his disciples. How would you like to develop a faith that God would consider to be amazing?

Allow these four principles from the seventh chapter of Luke to challenge you.

Get rid of your crutches

The centurion is an officer in charge of about a hundred men. He has a position of authority and influence. He is probably a God-fearing believer as shown by his support for the cause of the Jews.

His Jewish friends said that he helped build the synagogue. And because he cared deeply for the welfare of his slave, he is likely to be kind and merciful.

In those days, it would have been easier for someone in his position to simply dispose of the slave including having him killed as most masters would have done when a slave has run his usefulness.

But in approaching Jesus, he considered himself unworthy, so unworthy in fact that he had to go through his other Jewish friends.

> *V6 …the centurion sent friends to say to him: "Lord, don't trouble yourself, for I do not deserve to have you come under my roof. 7 That is why I did not even consider myself worthy to come to you.*

He did not rest on his own authority or power, or even his acts of goodwill towards the Jews, or his kindness. He did not trust in his own wealth, which he probably had, for the healing of his servant.

Instead, he came with a position of humility, and unworthiness. He came with nothing to lean on to.

Amazing faith will *never* come to the fore when there is something else that we can rely upon as our crutch.

Faith does not get to become amazing when we still have a contingency.

What is that thing that we are leaning on to that prevents us from stepping out in amazing faith?

Here in Australia, we have an excellent health care system which provides everyone, rich or poor, easy access to medicines and hospital care.

When we get sick, we typically do not have the opportunity for our faith to truly rise up out of desperation. Because we can depend on medicine and science. It is a crutch that we can lean on to.

I was just in my thirties when I received a bad report from a pap screening test. I was immediately sent for a cervical biopsy which confirmed the presence of abnormal cells that could lead to cancer if untreated.

The first step was to undergo laser treatment to burn the diseased cells.

Now, I could have just gone along with that. After all, the disease was just in its early stages and treatment was readily available.

But at that moment, I distinctly sensed a *call to halt* in my spirit.

Stop right there!

I remember a reprimanding within my soul for even entertaining the suggestion of this illness. The crutch of remedy was *right there.*

But why must I wait before things got really bad before I turned to God for healing? I decided I was going to hold on to God's promise from the very start. I prayed and fasted for an all-clear result.

When I went in for the laser treatment, the first thing the doctor needed to do was to examine me for the abnormal cells.

I told the doctor that I had been praying for a normal result. 'Well, let's see if your prayer worked,' she said.

She examined me but could not find any of the diseased cells! She had to call another doctor to examine me again to be sure. The second doctor confirmed the diagnosis. I was given the all clear and did not even have to get laser treatment.

This was close to two decades ago and I have been healthy since. I have well and truly thrown away that crutch.

The second point in developing amazing faith is very simply to…

Act on your faith

The centurion did not rest on his position, authority, influence, wealth or even his good works. He believed in Jesus and knew healing comes from Him. But he did not just sit there. His faith was not inactive. He acted.

> *3 The centurion heard of Jesus and sent some elders of the Jews to him, asking him to come and heal his servant.*

Faith that does *not* move into action, a faith that is dead – can never be amazing. As the apostle James said, faith is dead without action.

Now, the centurion had every reason not to act on this issue.

First, it was 'only' his slave who was sick.

Possibly indispensable? Maybe. But also because he was a Gentile and he could have excused in his mind that Jesus, a Jewish rabbi might not want to come to his house or respond to his request to heal his servant.

Sometimes we convince ourselves why we should not – before we even act! But these obstacles did not stop him from acting on his faith.

My husband, Rogelio turned 60 in December last year and I organized a surprise garden party at the beautiful Mt Tomah Botanical Gardens, an hour and a half drive up the mountains from Sydney.

But during this summer season in Australia, the bush fires were particularly bad.

On the day of his birthday party, there were reported brush fires in the area. But we decided to persevere, pray and keep believing for the best outcome!

On the way up, the smoke was getting thicker. Oh my. Were we going to turn back? We could have easily given up and allowed our faith to dwindle.

Yet we chose the opposite. We pressed on.

When we reached the beautiful garden up in the mountain, lo and behold, all around us were clear blue skies! We were sitting on top of the smoke far below!

So we did have a happy celebration that day. But if we did not act on our faith and turned back, all that would have been lost.

Faith that does *not* move into action, a faith that is dead – can *never* be amazing.

But the pinnacle of developing amazing faith is in the third point:

Completely trust in the Word

7 ....But say the word, and my servant will be healed.

Just say the word and it shall be done. How astounding that the centurion did *not* need Jesus to be physically present. He only needed His spoken word, and the centurion completely trusted and had full assurance that it would be done.

I don't know about you but my husband and I sometimes get into arguments over the GPS...especially our car GPS.

We argue about whether we should trust it.

So often, we would have it on but in addition to it, we would also have our Google maps active on my mobile. It's a GPS but we don't want to trust the direction it is giving us.

Now trouble happens when the car GPS gives us a different direction to the google maps on my mobile.

Which one are we going to trust now?

At that point, we need to make a decision because the reality is that we can only follow one, and which we follow, will determine how long we get to our destination or worse, whether we even *get* there.

In our Christian walk, we are faced daily with the choice of either embracing what God says – or, believing the deception of the world and the enemy of our soul, which we find leads to defeat and destruction.

We need to completely trust in the authority of the Word.

How can faith be amazing if we waver in accepting the promise?

The fourth and last step in developing amazing faith is to:

Expect amazing results

10 Then the men who had been sent returned to the house and found the servant well.

Many of us likely trust in the Word of God...*most* days. But probably *not enough* to expect **amazing results**.

Amazing faith expects amazing results. In our passage, the slave not only got healed, he got healed *instantly*.

When we completely take God at his word about who we really are, do we start imagining the amazing results in our lives?

Or, do we compromise and mentally prepare for a sensibly small outcome...or worse, expect a negative end and then get surprised when our prayers get answered instead? Where is the amazing faith in *that*?

Amazing faith expects amazing results.

I am a Star Wars fan. I have seen all nine movies.

In the movie 'Empire Strikes Back', Luke Skywalker was exiled on a planet to undergo training by Master Yoda to become a Jedi.

In one particularly memorable scene, Yoda directed Luke to lift his ship out of the swamp using The Force. Luke tried a few times and failed, complaining that Yoda was simply asking for the impossible. So the master lifted the ship himself. Luke exclaimed, *'I can't believe it!'*

And Master Yoda's immortal words of wisdom were, *'And that is why you failed.'*

We really need to rally our amazing faith to take the Lord at His word. To take His word about us and live in the fullness of this truth. Lord give us faith! Lord, make our faith **amazing**!

We need to get rid of our crutches – what we are holding on to for our security. We need to act on our faith.

We are to completely trust in the authority of God's word and what it says about us. And then we can expect *amazing results*.

Now here are some declarations that you could personally decree, to exercise your faith to *amazing* status today. Are you ready?

I am chosen!

I am a royal priest!

I am holy!

I am special!

I belong to God!

I am no longer in darkness!

I am in God's wonderful light!

I have received mercy!

I have everything I need to live a godly life!

I am called!

I have access to many great and precious promises!

I have a share in God's divine nature!

This is who you are. Now, rise up with a faith that amazes God.

The Powerful P in PURPOSE

35 Very early in the morning, while it was still dark, Jesus got up, left the house and went off to a solitary place, where he prayed. Mark 1:35

What is the powerful P that propels us to our true purpose?

The key that unlocks our purpose is **prayer**.

Without that P or prayer, PURPOSE is simply 'URPOSE'. U R only posing!

Leonard Ravenhill, writer of many books on prayer and revival made this direct and uncompromising statement:

"No man is greater than his prayer life. The pastor who is not praying is playing; the people who are not praying are straying. The pulpit can be a shop window to display one's talents; the prayer closet allows no showing off."

We need to apply that powerful P to keep us aligned and actively fulfilling our purpose.

But why is it the powerful P in purpose?

It is because PRAYER does four things in relation to our purpose...

Prayer REVEALS our purpose

> Proverbs 3:5,6 NKJV
> *5 Trust in the Lord with all your heart, And lean not on your own understanding; 6 In all your ways acknowledge Him, And He shall direct your paths.*

In the New International Version, it says, *'He will make your paths straight.'* In the New Living Translation, it says, *'He will show you which path to take.'*

Prayer is seeking God for His direction. Without it, we are without a compass. In our seeking, He reveals our purpose.

> *Jeremiah 33:3 Amplified Bible (AMP) 3 'Call to Me and I will answer you, and tell you [and even show you] great and mighty things, [things which have been confined and hidden], which you do not know and understand and cannot distinguish.'*

Do you want revelation about anything in your life, or about your purpose? You cannot have that revelation *without* prayer.

Usually, the Lord does *not* reveal our purpose in a single moment. It is typically a journey and a process in itself. That lack of clarity, leads us to persevere in prayer even more.

So, the next thing that prayer does is...

Prayer CLARIFIES our purpose

In Ephesians chapter 1, Paul prayed that the *'eyes of the hearts'* (NIV) or the *eyes of our understanding* (NKJV) will be enlightened to God's calling. Enlightened means 'opened up', or 'focused into clarity'. I like the way it is rendered in The Message:

> Ephesians 1:18,19 MSG
> *I ask—ask the God of our Master, Jesus Christ, the God of glory—to make you intelligent and discerning in knowing him personally, your eyes focused and clear, so that you can see exactly what it is he is calling you to do, grasp the immensity of this glorious way of life he has for his followers, oh, the utter extravagance of his work in us who trust him—endless energy, boundless strength!*

As we seek God continually in prayer, it is similar to when the camera lens gets adjusted into focus – our purpose becomes sharper and clearer. That revelation is energizing and propels us to start walking in that purpose.

But the work of prayer does not end there. We continue to pray because…

Prayer ESTABLISHES our purpose

In Mark 1:38 after Jesus prayed, He said to His disciples, *'Let us go somewhere else—to the nearby villages—so I can preach there also. That is why I have come.'*

If there is anyone whom we know was sure of His purpose, that would be Jesus. His purpose had been revealed and clarified, way back in the beginning at the time of the Fall.

And yet, He continues to pray. Not only because we draw power from prayer but because in relation to our purpose, prayer has the power to solidify, firm up and establish our purpose.

Proverbs 16:3 *Commit to the Lord whatever you do, and he will establish your plans.*

So now that through prayer we are established in our purpose, why must we still continue in prayer?

Because…

Prayer MAINTAINS our purpose

There are many believers who have known their purpose with great clarity and conviction, lived it out and yet *without* the pervading support of prayer, sadly left their original call.

Prayer will keep us in steadfast pursuit, in our journey of fulfilling our purpose. Prayer maintains our purpose. That is why we need to be engaged in prayer constantly.

Job 22:26,27 The Message
"You'll take delight in God, the Mighty One, and look to him joyfully, boldly. You'll pray to him and he'll listen; he'll help you do what you've promised.

So, four ways by which prayer radically orients us firmly to our purpose:

Prayer REVEALS, CLARIFIES, ESTABLISHES and MAINTAINS our purpose. Let us not get lost in our spiritual journey. Let's keep that powerful **P** (prayer) in our **Purpose**.

Are you a believer for the long haul?
Unpacking the marks of a great finisher

At Western Sydney University where I work, I analyze a lot of data and use this information to gauge performance.

One of the measures that we monitor is the attrition rate which is the proportion of students that drop out or discontinue their studies. At the university, the annual attrition rate is close to 20%. This means that 1 out of 5 drop out and do not complete their studies.

Understanding the tremendous undertaking of simply securing a university placement in the first place, you would wonder why students would decide to drop out.

But yes, students do…at a remarkable 20% of the time.

There are many reasons why students drop out, and some are understandable. But this high incidence illustrates that there are those who give up and fail to finish what they have started.

Are you a finisher?

Did you get a gym membership and follow through with your exercise plan beyond the first two months of the year?

Did you start a healthy diet and stick to it till you achieved your health goals?

Did you embark on a reading plan and remain on schedule to finish?

Did you start and finish cleaning up that wardrobe, drawer or room?

Did you start a business or project and follow through the difficult phases of start-up?

It is great to start but there is no real victory if we *do not* finish, especially in our Christian walk.

In the first chapter of 2 Thessalonians, we unpack the five marks of a great finisher.

The **first** is…

Growing faith

v3 'your faith is growing more and more…

The number one mark of a great finisher is a *growing* faith.

Our faith must continually be growing and expanding. Did you receive the Lord Jesus as your Savior? Great! But our faith must grow beyond the inception of our belief.

Our faith must awaken to the many truths of His nature – that He is good and faithful, that He provides, that He heals, is a source of strength, peace and healing, that He is an ever-present help in time of trouble, that He will never leave us nor forsake us.

It is in this growing faith in our Lord that we will be able to stand through the challenges of our journey and last through the long haul.

Over twenty years ago, we were barely a year migrating to Australia, when my father who lived in the Philippines died.

Our family has been separated from my dad for years. My parents broke up while I was still in my teens and my father resided with his second family.

I feel sad when I think about our falling away from him but I have no ill feelings towards my dad.

Upon learning about his death, I arranged to go home for his funeral. My biggest concern was his soul. I had already shared the gospel to the entire family, my faith was no secret. But I wondered, was he saved before he passed?

What a great consolation when my sister shared that a pastor was able to visit my father at his death bed to minister to him about the love and salvation in Jesus. Before he passed, my father responded with repentance and surrendered to his Savior!

Upon hearing this, I cried out loud with profound relief and joy. It was the only thing that mattered. And in that moment, my faith in the incredible grace and love of God just grew.

Whenever I see someone going his wayward way, my faith goes back to this story and remains stubborn that God in His love will always make a way.

This experience and many others like it will grow our faith for the long haul.

But we need to allow God to be present and work through our circumstances. In these situations when God is actively operating, our faith *will* grow.

The first mark of a great finisher is a growing faith.

The **second** one is…

Increasing love for one another

v3 'the love all of you have for one another is increasing.'

Some believers stop in their faith journey or become spiritually bankrupt because they experienced some kind of a falling out with another believer.

The person is hurt or offended by a fellow believer or even the pastor himself! Sometimes, the offense or disappointment is so great, that the believer leaves the church…or worse, falls away from the faith entirely.

What a sad state of affairs when this happens. Is it the offender's fault? Is it the fault of the one who took offense? Usually, it is somewhere in between. But it would have unlikely happened if our love for one another were increasing.

The best way to cover offense is love, *'for love covers a multitude of sins'*.

We need to love one another in increasing measure! A love that is patient and kind, considerate, and not boastful. A love that is not self-seeking, not easily angered and does not keep a record of wrongs. A love that protects and rejoices in the truth.

If we nurture this type of love within our spiritual community, we will be Christians for the long haul.

The second mark of a great finisher is an increasing love for one another.

The **third** mark is…

Perseverance and endurance in trial

V4 'your perseverance and faith in all the persecutions and trials you are enduring.'

Those who do not finish are those who give up in the face of difficulty. They give up without completing the very process that the Lord intended to develop the perseverance and endurance in the first place.

You will not build up your endurance by giving up at the 10-minute point of a 30-minute cardio. You won't have the endurance to run a 10-kilometre race if you can only do a 30-minute run on the treadmill.

Similarly, perseverance and endurance will not be developed without trials. The bigger the trial, the greater the endurance.

> Romans 5:33 *Not only so, but we also glory in our sufferings, because we know that suffering produces perseverance…*

> James 1:2-32 *Consider it pure joy, my brothers and sisters, whenever you face trials of many kinds, 3 because you know that the testing of your faith produces perseverance.*

We simply *cannot* separate trials from the building of perseverance and endurance. Through trials, you will build spiritual stamina that will make you persevere through the process and endure through the long haul.

So, rather than begrudging the testing, we need to trust God with the process that will build and strengthen our faith muscles.

The third mark of a great finisher is perseverance and endurance in trial.

The **fourth** mark is…

Hope of vindication and eternal glory

Sometimes trials seem to stretch far too long and there seems to be no end in sight.

The mark of the believer that will finish well is his unwavering hope in God.

This is about having that firm confidence in the One who does not slumber, whose arms are not too short to save, whose vindication is certain, whose love is unfailing and whose rescue comes on time.

> *6 God is just: He will pay back trouble to those who trouble you 7 and give relief to you who are troubled, and to us as well. This will happen when the Lord Jesus is revealed from heaven in blazing fire with his powerful angels. 8 He will punish those who do not know God and do not obey the gospel of our Lord Jesus. 9 They will be punished with everlasting destruction and shut out from the presence of the Lord and from the glory of his might 10 on the day he comes to be glorified in his holy people and to be marveled at among all those who have believed. This includes you, because you believed our testimony to you.*

Stand unwavering knowing your position in Christ. Recognize that you are a son and daughter brought by the precious blood of His Son. That pain and suffering does not for one second escape your Abba's attention.

If you as a parent will rise up to protect the suffering of your own children, will not the Almighty God, your Heavenly Father also come to your rescue? And if the respite does not come in the way that you imagine, there is still the ultimate hope of eternal glory to look forward to.

Understanding this truth will keep you strong for the long haul.

The fourth mark of a great finisher is hope of vindication and eternal glory.

The **fifth** mark is…

The residing and effectual power of God

One can have a growing faith, increasing love for others, they can even endure in trials with unwavering hope, but *without* the residing and effectual power of God, present in one's life, a Christian is not guaranteed to last for the long haul.

This is rendered more clearly in the Amplified Version,

> *v11 with [His] power fulfill every desire for goodness, and complete [your] every work of faith…*

What this verse is saying is that it is the **_power_** of God that fulfills or 'brings to fruition' (NIV) our acts of goodness and it is *His power* that enables us to complete every work of faith and righteousness.

That's why we are called to abide in Him (John 15). Because unless we do and unless we have the residing and effectual power of God working in us, His life-giving power will not be present. We will wither, and before we know it, break away.

But here is the revelation.

The power of God works with some raw material present. There has to be a *'desire for goodness'* for His power to fulfill and there must be *'works of faith'* for His power to complete.

Indeed, we are called to offer something on that altar. And that sacrifice, offered in faith, shall be rewarded by His residing power.

Five marks of a great finisher are: growing faith, increasing love for one another, perseverance and endurance in trials, hope of vindication and eternal glory, residing and effectual power of God.

Let us finish strong our DIVINELY DESIGNED EXTRAORDINARY LIFE.

[NB: All Bible quotes are from the New International Version (NIV) unless otherwise stated.]

The Corpuz Family at a wedding. Left to Right:
Aleli's daughter Abigail, husband Roger, son Richard, and Aleli

ALELI GRACE ANGELES–CORPUZ

Aleli Grace Angeles-Corpuz is a volunteer pastor at the Love of Jesus Christian Ministries, a family church based in the suburb of Glendenning in Sydney Australia where she has served since 1995 after migrating from the Philippines. She is married to Rogelio Corpuz and has two grown children, Richard Andrew and Ruth Abigail.

She also currently works at Western Sydney University as a statistician and data specialist. She has also worked at the state's transport department for two decades as well as at the Australian Bureau of Statistics for three years.

She and her husband love to travel. They have travelled to North America as far north as Canada and Alaska; Central America; South America; Europe; Greece and the Mediterranean area; Egypt; Israel; many parts of Asia including China, India and Japan; all around Australia and the Philippines; as well as Africa.

But her love for travel is very much secondary to her love for God. She met the Lord at 14 at a bible study in her high school. Her faith has sustained her through many challenges in her teenage years including a broken home, absent parents and the responsibility of looking after her young siblings at age 17.

CHAPTER 3

DIVINELY DESIGNED PATHWAYS

By Leni Hufana-Del Prado

FACING THE INEVITABLE WITH HOPE

Psalm 90:12 *"Teach me to number my days that I may present a heart of wisdom"*

Job 14:5 *"Since his days are determined, and the number of his month is with you and you have appointed limits that he cannot pass."*

As I turned on the television this morning and tuned in to CNN, as I normally do, I couldn't believe the news!

Together with the whole world, I was shocked at the passing on the basketball legend Kobe Bryant and his daughter Gianna.

It was incredibly surreal and somewhat creepy to think that someone who won the N.B.A's Most Valuable Player award (2007-2008 season), was also the N.B.A Finals' a top scorer, who had an impressive resumé – was now *dead* at a young age of forty-one years old.

People were jolted and appalled at the grim fate of Kobe Bryant and his daughter whom he fondly called "Gigi".

A few months prior to Kobe Bryant's tragic death, I had the opportunity to speak to a terminally ill woman whom I have known to be amiable and warm.

Every time I would see her, she would always be ready with a broad smile and was open to conversation.

When I learned of her sickness, I was given a burden by God, to pray and reach out to her, which I did.

I asked The Lord to give me a special time with her alone…and that's *exactly* what He did.

One day, I saw her sitting all alone in her, and felt a sudden nudge from the Holy Spirit that *this* was the time that God gave me to speak to her.

I stepped into her space and upon seeing me, she gave me that familiar broad smile – only this time, there was a look of sadness in her eyes.

After the pleasantries, the chat turned serious as she was somber with questions that bothered her about suffering and the after-life.

The conversation shifted into a topic that eventually opened her eyes, as the Holy Spirit led me into a discussion of faith through Jesus Christ.

As our time together progressed, by God's grace, there was a *definite shift* in the way she viewed her suffering and her future.

She said that she had been searching and asking God for answers. Well, God gave her His answer by opening her heart and mind to His salvation through Jesus Christ.

In our brief time together, she *did* surrender to Jesus and accepted Him as her personal Lord and Savior!

The passage in Psalm 90:12 and Job 14:5, take us to place in our lives where the brevity of life is *all too real.*

It is a place that the temporal such as material things, wealth, accolades, achievements and physical appearances are no longer important – and eternity becomes the **only** thing that matters.

There are facts that we can be sure of: 1) Our life here on earth will end at some point; 2) Our lives on earth are numbered and God determines that.

While we *do* have a responsibility to keep our bodies healthy, we cannot discount the fact that God is Sovereign and in control. His foresight is infallible. He determines when we arrive this planet, and when we leave this earth.

James 4:14 describes our lives are described as *"a mist that appears for a while and disappears."* And Psalm 39:4 describes life as *"fleeting".*

When someone close to us is sick or has passed away, we are faced with this fact – that life is indeed fleeting and like a mist.

Thus with sober judgment, we assess this person's life and hopefully, assess ours as well.

While we do think of the welfare of the family members we leave behind, we may wonder about the aftermath of the day we take that last breath. Let us be reminded that our lives matter to God, most especially our eternity.

His redeeming grace guarantees us a future of being with Him in paradise. What a wonderful promise of God!

Questions to Ponder:

Have you ever come face to face with death or know someone who has passed away?

What thoughts ran through your mind? What do you think will matter to you most during that time?

Scripture Reading:

John 3:16 says *"For God so loved the world that He gave His only Son, for whosoever believes in Him , shall not perish (eternal punishment) but have everlasting life."*

Prayer

Heavenly Father, thank You for your indescribable love that gives me hope. Thank you for giving me your Son Jesus, to die on the cross so that I could have an everlasting relationship with You. Thank You for the promise that when I put my faith in Jesus alone, believing in His authority to forgive sins as I repent of my own sins, and receive your forgiveness and cleansing, I am sure to be in paradise.

Jesus, be my Savior and the Lord of my life. I repent of my sins and surrender my life, my aspirations, and my will to You. Teach me to number my days that I may present a heart of wisdom. In the Mighty name of Jesus. Amen.

THE SPRING OF LIVING WATER

John 7: 38 *"He who believes in Me , as the Scripture said "From His innermost being will flow rivers of living water."*

Psalm 1: 2-3 *"but his delight is in the law of The Lord, and in His law, He meditates day and night. He will be like a tree planted by streams of water which yields its fruits in season. And its leaf does not wither.."*

Imagine yourself, walking through a piece of land that is barren and parched.

The skin on your back, down to your arms, aching as the sun beats down on your tiny frame and completely dries up the little moisture left in your throat.

Have you ever experienced that same barrenness in your spirit?

Barrenness takes on different forms.

Some will come in the form of being alone. They may experience this whether while living amongst lush greenery, or the midst of the busy, bustling city life. The silence of being alone can be deafening for those who experience this form of dryness.

Other forms may come in emptiness of mind and spirit.

There is a weariness like a tank that's running dry. There is no motivation in working, or maybe in serving God. There is a decided shift from joy to fatigue and it seems like one is carrying a heavy load.

When one starts to experience losing joy and work becomes more like an obligation, then there is the danger in experiencing total burn out.

I certainly have gone through times when serving in ministry became more of an obligation rather than a joy.

Indeed, there were times when I felt like I was carrying a *ton* of bricks!

I remember when I was leading a group of women, while at the same time doing the program for our small church almost every week to make it more interesting, and then sometimes preparing for a song , skits and dramas…and well, the props as well!

Problems with people arose and *oftentimes* would cause friction.

This drove me to withdraw and practically give up on ministry work. My world was getting smaller as my circle of friends within the church were finding it burdensome as well.

Stepping back and assessing things gave me a proper outlook on my motives and my relationship with God.

I had neglected that *one* thing that was more important to God, my *intimacy* with Him. After taking the time to be refreshed by God's word and have conversations with God, I felt invigorated and this brought back the joy of my salvation.

I had been thirsty even while in ministry and had forgotten to drink from the Spring of Living Water.

You may be going through a dry spell in your spirit. Perhaps life has become mundane and maybe an emptiness is cast over your mind.

Don't let it take root. Joy is found *in* God's presence.

Remember that joy can be restored by God. Recall the joy when you first met Jesus.

Crying out to God helped me overcome the joy which had been lost, as well as asking Him for forgiveness for the sins that I had committed.

Delight yourself in His Word. Jesus *is* the Spring of Living Water, the Source of our strength, our joy and our blessed hope.

Jesus, came to earth to suffer and die for our sins so that people could get right with God. God has placed a vacuum in our hearts to search for Him and that vacuum can only be filled with Jesus Christ.

Questions to Ponder:

Are you going through spiritual barrenness? Have you placed your faith in the only source of Joy?

Be encouraged by Scripture that will bring back that spring in your step.

Prayer

I come to you with a searching heart, asking You, dear Jesus to fill me with Your kind of joy, and my thirst to be quenched by You alone.

CROSSROADS

> Jeremiah 6:16 *"Thus says The Lord 'Stand by the roads and look, and ask for the ancient paths, where the good way is; and walk in it, and find rest for your souls.'"*

Oftentimes, during lazy afternoons, I recall the times that would transport me back in time to my life 30 years ago.

In my reverie, I recall having crossroads in my life, whether it was a decision to leave behind relationships or a lifestyle – *or* having to face an unknown future.

I left the Philippines completely unprepared to face the future.

I knew that it would entail a serious life, perhaps quiet and mundane compared to what I had in Manila. I wondered whether I was ready for that kind of life.

Before I left, I *did* have some propositions to be an actress on the big screen and be included in a series on television.

I loved the limelight. I was modelling then, frequented discos and had a few stints in acting.

So, when I decided to leave *everything* behind, that was the kind of life I was turning my back on.

But my mind was pretty set on this new adventure of *quieting down*.

In hindsight, I praise God for taking me *away* from all the noise.

My parents, sister and I happened to stumble upon a quaint Filipino-American church.

Upon much reflection, I knew that God had called me *back to Him*.

Through this church, I learned to love God's Word. I formed new friendships that gave me a different perspective in life. There was indescribable joy in this new found freedom, freedom from sin – that gave me an unexplained calmness in my heart.

In the Old Testament, there was an opportunity for wisdom in Judah when they were at a place of sin. Jeremiah, the prophet told them that there was wisdom in looking back at the examples of their forefathers and their history with God – how God took them, cared for them and taught them: divine lessons, the path of repentance, reconciliation, holy fear and the love of God.

Prayer

Heavenly Father, teach us to look at the examples You have us given us in Your Word and to learn from them. Teach us to look to the ancient paths that lead back to You, and to stay on the straight and narrow as we are faced with the crossroads of our lives.

FEARFULLY AND WONDERFULLY MADE

Psalm 139 :13-16 *"For You formed my inward part; You wove me in my mother's womb, I will give thanks to You, for I am fearfully and wonderfully made; My frame was not hidden from You, When I was made in secret, And skillfully wrought in the depths of the earth; Your eyes have seen my unformed substance."*

An intelligent and fresh university graduate came to visit my husband and me one day, who had pre-conceived ideas regarding the origin of life and everything on the planet.

I was hesitant whether I should talk to him about how great God is and His intelligent design of the universe, and do my best to prove to him that his theories were wrong.

I didn't know if I had all my facts straight regarding historical evidence, and I was wary because I didn't know whether he would react or argue about how right he was.

Meanwhile, I prayed and kept praying, hoping that he would join me and tell me that he would like to accept Jesus as his Lord and Savior after going through the tract.

After about an hour, he approached me with some questions which he put forward. He was respectful and genuinely wanted answers to his queries.

God put these verses from Psalm 139 in my heart and the more the read it, the more I was moved to worship Him and focus on His attributes, His splendor, His power, the Creator EL ELOHIM.

There are just so many young minds with a load of questions like this young man did. Some may be cynical and sometimes we're faced with scoffers who won't listen to reason and whatever historical data you put in front with them.

I watched a video of a young man who was about 5 ft 5 inches, white, blond hair with blue eyes. He was going around a university campus asking questions like, "What if I tell you that I'm a black 6-foot woman, what would you say?"

I was completely astounded that almost all their answers where similar! Not wanting to offend, most replies were: "Well, if that's what you think, then that's what you are."

I didn't know whether to laugh or just worry about how the world has spiraled into a mindset that removes TRUTH and the teaching that dictates that "what you feel, is what you are."

A mindset like this will dictate how they think and how they live.

If this is the thinking of the next generation, then imagine what direction they will be headed for, since these will be the mindsets of the next generation of leaders of the country.

Sometime in our lives, we learn about the complexities of the human anatomy. The eyes, for example are intricately designed to bring most of the information we see, to the brain.

Have we considered intelligent design all around us, and its Designer?

Have you considered that every human is unique? Genetics has proven that.

Can we honestly say that we were merely created by a series of random explosions or circumstance?

We can search all day on the internet, but yet miss out on how great God is and that we are created by a skillful and intelligent designer who is unlike any other and who clearly comes before any human, or any life in the universe.

Because of His divine creation and all its uniqueness and grandeur, we look to God with reverence.

What is even more mind-blowing is God's lavish, furious love for us – His created beings, with whom He desires to have a relationship.

In reality, we are but a speck in the vastness of the universe, yet He made us with so much care and gave us a purpose to live.

Having seen therefore His creation, we are held accountable before God. In Romans 1:20 (ESV) it says *"For his invisible attributes, namely, his eternal power and divine nature, have been clearly perceived, ever since the creation of the world, in the things that have been made. So they are without excuse."*

Prayer

Heavenly Father, after seeing and experiencing the beauty of your creation, we marvel at who You are and what You have done. We bow the knees in honor and praise, thanking You for loving us and giving us a hope and a future by bringing us to salvation in Jesus Christ.

STANDING ALONE

Matthew 5:14 (ESV) *"You are the light of the world. A city set on a hill cannot be hidden."*

Matthew 5:16 (ESV) *"in the same way, let your light shine before others, so that they may see your good works and give glory to your Father who is in heaven."*

2 Chronicles 16:9 (ESV) *"For the eyes of The LORD run to and fro throughout the whole earth, to give strong support to those whose heart is blameless toward him."*

I think about times in people's lives that have created an impact in my walk with The Lord.

There are people who never looked back on their calling in spite of the many stumbling blocks that the enemy placed along their path. They stood up to righteousness.

One of them is my husband Patrick.

He always had a desire to teach and train young believers how to deepen their faith and trust in the Lord. He trains leaders of a church and leads them to maturity and submission under the headship of Jesus.

I remember during our earlier years as believers.

He was around 28 years old and worked for one of the top pharmaceutical companies in the world.

His struggles stemmed from going against company norms and practices, the norm being taking doctors to clubs or sleazy spas or KTVs where they mingled with young women.

He stood up to the norm in the sales force, his bosses and colleagues which would cause friction and even potential termination. But He did it because he loved God, and us, his family.

He fought against temptations even from women within the company who propositioned him to a sexual encounter. As shocking as it was about how women could be so bold, Patrick chose the high road by refusing to be engaged in any activity that would compromise his faith.

Despite all these things that satan had put in his way to make him trip, stumble and fall, my husband remained faithful to God and is still faithfully serving Him today.

Standing up for God and standing up against the world system, do bring honor to Him. His attributes of Holiness and power are on display for the world to see, creating impact in the workplace.

Because Patrick stood alone in making hard choices, people who were once "closet Christians" came out from hiding and made that decision to stand up and be counted as well.

He was even able to create a small bible study group in his office and became the first in the company who was sent on a regional role.

When he finally retired from that company, his good name and reputation remained intact and is presently being used mightily for God's kingdom.

How wonderful that some of the women who attended his bible studies then, are now in the women's discipleship group which I have the privilege of leading.

When we read Mathew 5:14-16, we think of our lives as being light to a dark world, a world that doesn't know Jesus. We can be influencers for Jesus by standing up for God to show them His salvation and His righteousness.

By being lights to a fallen world, we can show them the way out of the darkness through the work of God's love in our lives and as the Holy Spirit reveals sin in their lives.

2 Chronicles 16 is a story of Asa, King of Judah who took treasures from the house of the LORD and gave them to a heathen king, Ben-hadad, King of Aram, asking Ben-hadad to break the latter's covenant with Israel, and instead to take King Asa's side. Ben-hadad agreed and attacked the towns of Israel.

In so doing, King Asa had put his trust in the King of Aram, instead of relying on His fathers' covenant with God.

This angered the LORD because King Asa relied on the king of Syria and not on the LORD.

Have you ever experienced having to make hard choices in the company you work for? By doing so, did you take the high road by standing alone in a decision that was against the normal practice?

May you be proven to be a faithful servant of God even under tough circumstances and making tough choices.

Prayer

Heavenly Father, there are times in my life when I have the opportunity to choose what is right in Your eyes, and oftentimes I fail.

Teach me, through the example of faithful followers that it is possible to choose to be on Your side no matter the consequences.

Help me take this step of faith and stand up for You, even when faced with tough choices. May we always look to Jesus who is the Author and Perfecter of our faith.

<hr />

STARTING OVER

Isaiah 43:18-19 *"Remember not the former things, nor consider the things of old. Behold I am doing a new thing; now it springs forth, do you not perceive it? I will make a way in the wilderness and rivers in the desert."*

1 John 1:9 *"If we confess our sins, He is faithful and just to forgive us our sins and to cleanse us from all unrighteousness."*

When I was a young adult, I made a decision to do things *my* way, seek life outside the comfort of home, which I regarded at that point as unspirited.

I felt that my simple life was so *boring* and uneventful, so I sought for a more exciting existence.

I joined a beauty pageant that allowed me to meet the rich and famous, and the city's most beautiful people during those times.

I left my family and soaked in the pleasures of the world…and as I did that, I turned my back on my Lord.

There are many stories in one's life that involve wrong decisions, regrets, failures.

Oftentimes we try and resuscitate the past and relive it, causing us to regret living in it all the more.

There are many events in my life that I regret, mostly the wrong decisions that I've made, that caused me to stumble in my walk with God.

We hear pastors talk about living a life without regrets.

Several questions raced through my mind: *"What if we did live a life of regrets, how do get back on track? How do we go back to God's good pleasure? Will God ever accept me back?*

One thing that I missed during those times I was living in that carnal world, was the peace and joy that I had experienced with Jesus.

I truly missed Him.

The material life brought only temporary pleasures, void of anything substantial. And I just ended up heartbroken.

Thankfully, I left that life, and went back to rejoin my family who had migrated to the U.S.

We joined a church. A Christian lady whom I'd just met then, brought me to their bible study group of single young ladies and men. Pretty soon, I was discipled by a young couple, and with their help, I was back on track.

Isaiah 43:18-19 reminds us of how God makes a way for us to start over, even during dark times in our past. When one comes to Him in repentance and surrender, He leads us to a new life of fresh anointing.

He leads us to start anew and allows us leave the past behind us.

There is hope for anyone who comes to Jesus in complete surrender. The prophetic passage that Isaiah wrote to exiled Israel, gives light on the work He will do in us and through us.

It is a call that if one is stuck in failures, in sin and discouragement, one will never go forward to the new things that God wants us to do.

God calls us, rescues us, and know that He will make a road in the wilderness, and rivers in the desert.

Prayer

Heavenly Father, thank You for giving me a another chance to live a new life in Jesus. Thank You for taking me out from the shackles of sin and putting me back in Your arms.

Thank You for Your forgiveness and showing me the rivers in the desert. Help me to live a life of surrender and purpose by the power of the Holy Spirit through Jesus Christ.

AUTHENTICITY IN OUR LIFE

Hebrews 4:12 *"For the word of God is living and active , sharper than any two edge sword, piercing to the division of soul and spirit , of joints and of marrow, and discerning the thoughts and intentions of the heart."*

Psalm 51:10-12 *"Create in me a pure heart Oh God, and renew a steadfast spirit within me. Do not cast me from your presence or take your Holy Spirit from me. Restore to me the joy of my salvation."*

2 Corinthians 10:5 *"We demolish arguments and every pretension that sets itself up against the knowledge of God and we take every thought captive to make it obedient to Christ."*

Social media is a means for people to virtually congregate, get world events or local news, for research, to buy and sell and advertise.

My daughter-in-law Nikki, who was once a celebrity, has thousands of followers. Media people followed her on social media, sometimes exploited gossip to post fake news, which they use to post about her life.

As an influencer, she was offered by companies to display their products online in exchange for a stylish, classy and pricey fare.

Normally, young women would easily be seduced to something this easy to acquire, because it would be a no-brainer to agree to something as simple as this.

And yet, she turned them down!

I was baffled, yet somehow I knew the reason why.

She shied away from the limelight and chose to live a quiet life away from the glitz and glamour. She saw through all the pretense, seduction and worldliness…and she chose wisely.

What we see on social media is most often just a façade.

Most often it's what people want to project rather than who they really are.

Stripping off the veil is quite difficult to do when one has acquired layers of it. However, the ones who see the real person are those who are closest to them – like their family.

Children sometimes give the most honest observations of their parents. Their comments strike a chord in us that allow us those moments in time to get real. Being authentic is stripping away the veil, and most often, layers of it. And at times it calls for a lot or tears.

There is also getting real with God. The attributes of God include His ability to read hearts, His ability to judge our attitudes and to bring them to the surface.

We understand that He knows us more than we know ourselves. We may be an expert at hiding our real self, but with God everything is laid bare.

Yet, there are those who are followers of Jesus who live a *double life*.

Some may even be in ministry work. These people think that they can get away with sin but by doing so, reject God's omniscience and power.

There is a layer deep down in the recesses of our hearts and minds that only God sees.

To live in authenticity means a peeling away of layers of pretense and lies even to ourselves. It involves renouncing and rejecting our shameful ways, correcting our wrong thinking and getting right with God. It is knowing that *nothing* is hidden from God.

This reminds me of the story of King David in 2 Samuel 11. While kings led their armies to war, he chose to stay in the comfort of the palace.

While he stayed behind, he saw a beautiful woman bathing. This sin of lust led to a progression of a series of sinful acts. The lies and schemes to cover up his shameful sin caused the death of his loyal soldier Uriah, followed by a confrontation by the prophet Nathan.

The consequences of David's sin included the death of David son, among others.

In Psalm 51, we read of his repentant heart and how he desired to get right with God.

We are called to live an authentic life and repel hypocrisy and by doing so, we become attractive for people to come to know the One True God whom we serve. We become models of God's transforming power and we will not be held captive by the schemes of the enemy.

Questions to Ponder:

Is there anything in your life, perhaps in your thought life that needs to be renounced and repented of before God?

Prayer

Heavenly Father, show me my heart and if there is any grievous way in me, I repent of this sin and ask for forgiveness. Create in me a pure heart and renew a steadfast spirit within me.

GODLINESS IN THE MIDST OF TRIALS

2 Corinthians 4:17 *"For this momentary affliction is preparing for us an eternal weight of glory beyond all comparison."*

James 1: 12 *"Blessed is the man who remains steadfast under trial , for when he has stood the test he will receive the crown of life , which God has promised for those who love him."*

My husband and I have had the privilege of knowing this young couple, Aldrin and Gina, who have had an unswerving affection and adoration for God.

Before Aldrin came to know the Lord, he was a young waiter at a quaint restaurant inside a university campus and Gina, a young Christian woman was working in a supermarket.

Aldrin is reserved and always respectful of others and Gina until today, is industrious, gregarious and warm.

She shared the gospel with him and introduced him to the elders of the church after bible studies. He soon committed his life under the Lordship of Jesus Christ.

Three years later, Aldrin and Gina were wed in a simple but beautiful ceremony. Meanwhile, my husband served as an elder, and I had the privilege of teaching the women of this growing church. So this couple whom we helped mentor and lead, opened their hearts and home to us.

They both were actively serving in church and walked closely with Jesus when Aldrin was diagnosed with Nasopharyngeal Carcinoma.

The tumor inside his nose rapidly took over his cheek, his eyes and his whole body. After his chemo and radiation treatments, his face and body became unrecognizable, and he weighed a meager forty kilos from his original weight of seventy-five kilos!

His once roundish, handsome face became gaunt and he lost all his dark curly hair. His eyes lost their luster and he even became cross-eyed.

Yet his faith became even stronger than ever and both of them became even more determined to serve the Lord with the same passion and perseverance.

His malaise and pain didn't stop him from playing the guitar on Sundays even when he couldn't speak in front when he lost his voice. He even watered the plants at church and encouraged the young people to continue serving.

At clinic visits, while waiting to be called in to see a doctor, he shared the gospel to people. Many of those who were sick and dying came to the saving power of the Lord Jesus. He was content with that and he found joy in serving God.

On May 19, 2018, he succumbed to cancer while on vacation together with his wife, his son and people from the church.

My husband and I were struck with disbelief. We thought he was getting better!

Questions raced through my mind like "How could God allow something bad to happen to a godly man? Why did He allow suffering and pain to dwell in someone who was faithful?"

We were both filled with sorrow and as we heard Gina's wails, out of a broken heart. It is beyond our finite minds to think that they went through a turbulent path.

Since we lived abroad, we were helpless. We sought to comfort her while we tried to make sense of what happened.

It wasn't only King David that was after God's own heart.

There was also Aldrin. He was broken as God loves the broken in spirit and a contrite heart. Aldrin and Gina have set an example for people who are suffering.

Their faith had given them a deep love for God, with surrendered hearts.

The apostle Paul was very familiar with suffering. In 2 Corinthians 11:16-28, he listed the afflictions he went through such as being in an out of prison frequently, flogged more severely, exposed to death several times. He was lashed, pelted with stones, beaten with rods, shipwrecked three times, he even spent a day and a half in the open sea.

Paul went through dangerous cities and met dangerous people. Oftentimes he was without sleep, without food and water or even clothing. Yet he was still concerned for the people of God. His suffering didn't stop him from praising God or living for Him.

He was still driven by love for God and His people, and by gratitude.

Suffering exposes our hearts. It is a wake up call to us and even when we don't understand it, it forces us to look at the crossroads and choose our reaction to it.

It takes us to a place where we have to face it squarely, as it takes us to who God is.

As we read 2 Corinthians 4:17 and James 1:12, we are encouraged and reminded that those who are in Christ, though faced with affliction, and what seems like never ending stress from work, people, and circumstances – we can look forward to a safety net, that is our eternal inheritance where there no longer will be any sickness, or corruption.

Questions to Ponder:

When you are faced with tremendous trials, even those that seem too huge to carry, what is the first thing that you do?

Do you take it up with God first? Do you try and solve it yourselves first? Do you seek Him? Or do you turn away from Him? Do you look at the blessings of comfort from people God sends your way to help you financially and emotionally? How does suffering shape your faith?

Prayer

Heavenly Father, when we go through the valleys in our lives and especially the ones that cause so much pain, may we be drawn to You and Your attributes like mercy, compassion, comfort and forgiveness. Cause us to seek Jesus, rely on You and hang on to Your promises in Your word.

WHAT DRIVES YOU?

John 16:8 *"And He when He comes, will convict the world concerning sin, righteousness and judgment."*

1 Corinthians 15:33 *"Do not be deceived "bad company ruins good morals."*

Genesis 13:10 *"Lot looked around and saw that the whole plain of the Jordan toward Zoar, was well watered, like the garden of The Lord, like the land of Egypt. 11. So Lot chose for himself the whole plain of Jordan and set out toward the east."*

"When Holy God draws near in true revival, people come under terrible conviction of sin. The outstanding feature of spiritual awakening has been the profound consciousness of the Presence and holiness of God." ~Henry Blackaby.

I've had the opportunity to step back and reflect on the teachings of Chuck Swindoll (Insight for Living) regarding the life of Abraham and Lot in the book of Genesis.

It was a poignant lesson on the urgency of gaining wisdom through the Holiness of God in relation to having strong convictions.

Stories in Genesis 18 about the conversation that Abraham had with the angels and the Lord regarding the impending punishment on Sodom and Gomorrah resonated *deeply* within me.

At the time of this writing, it is the second month of the Covid-19 pandemic, and this period has given me new perspectives in life and deeper, *much* deeper insights into the attributes of God.

This deeper appreciation *and* understanding are what drive me to serve Him more and drive me to develop a new outlook on life.

There was still self-will in me, revealed thru this lockdown period.

I realized that I couldn't do much of anything now, in this time of Covid. It seemed that the things that I had wanted to do and yearned for, were stripped.

I have been left with staying at home, spending more time with my husband and God, abiding, surrendering and giving up my self-indulgence to serving others.

As the lesson on depravity, the overflowing cesspool of Sodom continued, Chuck Swindoll conveyed the urgency of having convictions.

Convictions are strong, deep inner principles on **morality, integrity, ethics and faith** that drives what we do, how we think, and how we regard people and the world.

Of course, it requires authenticity and self awareness and they become more powerful when they are presented to God.

My husband shared his convictions that he brought forth before God. He stood on the principles of having strong moral convictions and faith in God.

Now we look back in hindsight at our life together as husband and wife as he shared glimpses of what his life was like in the firm where he worked.

He stood up to his boss who had wanted to bring the whole team to a sleezy bar. He stood up to women who had propositioned him at work and refused to be put in a compromising situation. He raised the bar of morality in his office, no matter the cost and became like a beacon of godliness and leadership.

He set up a bible study at his office, and his life became a credible witness of God's transforming power.

Convictions drive people to stand for righteousness and cause them to willingly take the consequences for standing firm.

Reading and studying the life of Lot, made me understand the resemblance of a life *without* convictions.

Lot chose for himself a land that was well-watered. It was described as a land like the garden of Eden (Genesis 13:10). Being attracted to a life of leisure and comfort drove him to live in that wicked city.

God brought down His judgment on that city that burned down the twin cities to the ground with fire and brimstone (Genesis 19).

As toxic fumes contaminate the air, closely associating ourselves with the wisdom of this world contaminates our thinking, our attitudes and our lifestyle until we grow numb to the things of God and to God Himself.

There are times when God stops us on our tracks to draw us back to Himself. I have better understood why we go thru valleys and storms in our lives because sometimes, they point us in the right direction, back to Himself.

I am inspired by those who have walked faithfully with God and have stood the tests and the storms that have come their way. They have finished this race well and are enjoying their eternal inheritance of being with Him in heaven.

Questions to Ponder:

Do you have convictions of your own that compel you to live a life that is led by the Holy Spirit? Have you brought them before God?

May the Holiness and the power of the Living Word teach us to lay down strong convictions to drive us to live a life that is well lived for God.

Prayer

Dear God, teach us to have strong convictions to help drive us in the right direction, to help stop us in our tracks, and to direct us to a path that leads to a life of abundance in Jesus.

***

EVERY BREATH WE TAKE

Deuteronomy 8:10-11 *"When you have eaten and are satisfied, praise the LORD your God for the good land He has given you". 11 Be careful that you do not forget The LORD your God, failing to observe His commands, His laws and decrees that I am giving you this day."*

1 Thessalonians 5:18 *"give thanks in ALL circumstances, for this is God's will for you in Christ Jesus."*

I vividly remember this familiar prayer before meals as a young girl: *"God is great, God is good, let us thank Him for our food. Amen."*

Praying this kind of prayer was *so* mechanical that we just prayed for the heck of it, because we were hungry and simply wanted to eat.

I also learned to thank God at night before bedtime, and yes it was practically the same prayer because as I prayed, my eyelids were heavy, and I just wanted to hit the pillows and catch some zzzs.

These were the kinds of prayer that I was accustomed to. They were familiar and quick. It didn't need pondering.

But when I met the Lord Jesus and understood the essence of prayer and how it could be like a fragrant offering to the Lord...it totally changed my viewpoint on it!

Do I take for granted all the temporal provisions from God?

Do I and must I forget His divine providence, His protection, His answers to prayers, His encouragement, His divine lessons that come my way?

I have learned that the antidote to complaining and self-glory is being *grateful*.

Gratefulness is an attitude that gives honor to the One from whom all blessings come from.

Oftentimes, it is neglected especially when we do enjoy the limelight and are given that chance to shine wherever we are. We can so easily be like the Israelites during the time when they were about to cross the Jordan to the land God was giving them, after the giving of the Ten Commandments.

Moses reminded them to keep the commandments close to their hearts and to follow them. He also reminded them of what God did for them and why He led them through the wilderness for *forty years*.

They needed to be humbled, since they were grumbling all the time, ungrateful that they were rescued from The Egyptians.

The Lord had fed them manna and their clothes did not wear out nor did their feet swell the entire forty years (Deuteronomy 8:4). Moses was telling them that the Lord was now bringing them into a good land – a land with brooks and streams and deep springs gushing out into valleys and hills (Deut.8:6) and so he reminded them of how good the Lord was to them.

When we are given honor in the work we have done, or being applauded because of our efforts in what we do, do we give back the honor and glory due God?

In Deuteronomy 8:17-18 says "You may say to yourself, 'My power and strength of my hands have produced wealth for me. But remember the LORD your God, for it is he who gives you the ability to produce wealth…'".

The antidote to self-glory is really a sober judgment of oneself, being *thankful* to God for the abilities He gave us, and for allowing people to see your worth.

When I was given success in a task, the natural inclination of my heart was to tell myself that I had sacrificed so much, and I had exerted so much effort to make this job successful.

What I failed to consider was that it was God who had given me the ability, the clarity of mind, the peace in my heart, the people to encourage me, and a wealth of experiences and learnings – that resulted in my success.

Failure to honor God is exactly the characteristic of this pop-culture. It is a spiral downwards to moral depravity.

May we be aware of this natural inclination of man and turn the tables so that we can be *grateful* in our hearts and honor God as He deserves.

On the other hand, when things *don't* turn out the way we desire, do we thank the Lord for that as well?

Paul told the church in Thessalonica to be joyful always, to pray continually, and to give thanks in *all* circumstances.

Sometimes, I fail to consider that *every breath* I take is a blessing. The air we breath is free and it expands our lungs, promotes wellness and makes our blood circulate in our bodies. It reminds us that we are still alive!

We may be going thru testing and heavy trials, yet we can still be *grateful* as we are encouraged by His promises. He might send people to encourage you, or give you insight into His word and send some form of help.

There are numerous testimonies of believers whom God has done favors for, and from which you could draw from, aside from those in the scriptures and those whom He sends to counsel you.

Let us rejoice and be thankful in all circumstances knowing that we have a God who is living and actively involved in the lives of the ones He loves. His hand is never too short to help us, nor is He deaf, that He wouldn't listen to us.

Prayer

Heavenly Father, we give you all the glory and honor you deserve. May we always be reminded of the events in our lives and the examples of those in Your Word that encourage, and that teach us to be *grateful* in *all* circumstances.

Remind us of Your attributes which we easily forget. When we rise in the morning, remind us of the precious air we breath, the magnificent creation that's displayed before me, and make me consider Your work and praise You.

Teach me to develop an attitude of gratefulness and by doing so have a joyful attitude that others would see and that points to Jesus, the Author and Perfecter of my faith.

OVERCOMING THE DARK TIMES

Psalm 56:3 *"When I am afraid, I put my trust in you."*

Isaiah 41:13 *"For I am The Lord your God who takes hold of your right hand and says to you, Do not fear, I will help you."*

1 Peter 5:7 *"Cast all your anxiety on him because He cares for you."*

As I write this devotion, the world is in darkness as it is saturated in this pandemic called COVID-19, a new corona virus that has taken over our lives, our health, our businesses.

It started in Wuhan, China and has spread rapidly all over the globe at an unprecedented rate.

I am sure nobody is ignorant of this since it has cost many lives especially of the frontliners like doctors and nurses.

As they painstakingly carry out their duties, they are at a higher risk of acquiring the dreaded disease.

Countries like Italy, Europe, China and the Philippines are all on lockdown, and even the citizenry is not free to move around.

Malls in most countries are closed, and curfew hours are observed in hope to of curbing the virus's spread.

The worst is watching videos of hospitals overwhelmed with patients, hearing of other patients on the floor dying, because they couldn't get tested. It is like a freakish tale or horror movie that I'd seen in movies a few years back and **it is scary**.

I have questions that are running through my mind at the moment such as…

"Why is this happening?"

"What is God trying to tell us?"

"When will this all go away?"

"Will I still be alive? Will my husband? My kids?"

I myself, at times, have this fear of COVID, but getting down on my knees and praying fervently, lifting my questions and concerns and reading His Word, I am encouraged and there is a certain stillness that I feel, a peace that only God can give.

With this time that is given to me to reflect and study His word, along with the videos that are sent to me daily by the church community, to encourage me, I know that I have the responsibility to pray fervently for the nations.

I have read and re-read, prayed this prayer of Anne Graham Lotz which she prayed during "The National Day of Prayer" last March 15, 2020. This prayer had so deeply affected me in such a way that I internalized it and posted it to the ladies group that I lead, and to my family.

She stood in the gap, fervently prayed for forgiveness on behalf of the nation, asked our God for His mercy, repented of the sins of the people, which she named and confessed.

As we stand in the gap for the nations, and pray for people, let ours be a prayer of repentance, and a prayer that will move the heart of God.

Now that the Philippines is on lockdown and people are at home, we have no other recourse but to spend time with each other.

Before the lockdown, there wasn't much time to be with each other. Now we are faced with opportunities to reset and transform our lives, and our relationships – to a higher level of understanding, acceptance and camaraderie.

Technology is being used for work, to have face-to-face time with family members across the globe, to pray and share the gospel of Jesus, to spread warnings and news on the outbreak, to get the latest on the medicines being developed in other countries, and to come together for a bible study.

Lives are changed.

We are now made conscious of a higher level of hygiene that we've neglected for so long, we're more conscious of the well-being of the elderly and the kids.

We are becoming aware of that we need to take care of the environment, to look around us and to be grateful for God's creation.

We are made aware of our own mortality as death stares us in the face and we reflect on the reality that it's only a matter of time.

As we think on these things, we realize who hold the keys to life and death and who is the only one that can judge the living and the dead. From this, comes wisdom, the urgency and the fervency to pray.

We realize that everything and every event culminates in the mercy of God, His sovereignty, His timing, His omniscience, His omnipotence, His holiness, His power and His grace.

Questions to Ponder:

How would you react to an event that shakes you to the core? Would you spiral into depression or choose to just surrender and put your or trust in the Lord?

Doesn't the track record of the faithfulness of God speak to you?

As the world is gripped with fear and anxiety, I pray that we be a light to the darkness and show them their hope in Jesus.

Our anxieties we simply cast on Him because as Peter says in 1 Peter 5:7 *"…He cares for you."*

Prayer

Lord God, as I meditate on Your Word, give me the peace that surpasses all understanding.

May I look at Your attributes and Your promises instead, to reassure me that You are totally in control. Sometimes, things in our lives bring fear and sometimes we can be imprisoned by them, because the enemy continues to create havoc in our minds.

I ask you to please still my mind and protect it from the darting arrows of the enemy. Help me to rise above it and continue my walk with you, Jesus.

THE UPPER ROOM

Hebrews 10:24-25 *"and let us consider how we may spur one another on toward love and good deeds, 25 not giving up meeting together, as some are in the habit of doing, but encouraging one another -and all the more as you see the Day approaching"*

Proverbs 27:17 *"As iron sharpens iron, so one person sharpens another".*

It is a privilege and an honor to serve in the ministry that God has purposed for me – serving amongst wonderful women of faith.

Through the guidance of the Holy Spirit of God, I help lead and guide women to strengthen their faith, mentor and point them in the direction of Jesus Christ, the Author and Perfecter of our faith.

Some are now leading and mentoring other women. I am also being led and guided by my small group leaders who are godly and men and women full of faith.

My husband and I have had the opportunity to be under the tutelage of spiritual parents who have patiently led us to deeper faith by being grounded in the Scriptures after which led us to being used by God ourselves.

The beauty in community lies in the example of the first disciple group leader, Jesus Christ. He led His disciples, taught them the deep things of God, opened their eyes to their true condition before God and showed them Himself – as the Messiah Who would suffer and die for the sins of the world.

He encouraged them concerning the kingdom of God. Though He witnessed their distrust, and human errors, He guided them with so much patience and care, pointing out the errors of their ways and He lovingly corrected them.

He led by example.

When the disciples gathered together in the upper room in Acts 1, they recounted all that had happened after they had seen Jesus ascend into Heaven from the Mount of Olives.

They went back to Jerusalem and went to the upper room. They all joined together praying constantly, along with the women and the earthly family of Jesus.

Peter spoke with the words from the book of Psalms and recaptured their time with Jesus and what the scriptures revealed concerning the fulfillment of prophecies concerning Him.

The birth of the church came about during the time of the introduction of the Holy Spirit of God on the day of Pentecost in Acts 2.

The gathering of a community of believers helps us have a sense of belonging, a place where there is encouragement through the study of the Holy Scriptures, through worship and prayer.

We have small groups within the church community that is also a safety net for people go to.

My husband and I attend a small group, and I also lead a small group of women. It is such a blessing to be able to **lead** and **be led**.

The community helps one to love God deeply and shows one that it is possible to have a *victorious life*. I certainly have grown through the years of being in a church and a small group.

It is a refreshing time to being accountable, to be lovingly corrected, as we are inclined stumble and fall as well.

Questions to Ponder:

Do you belong in a church? How about joining a small group that you can be a part of?

Joining a small group could be a huge part of your spiritual journey, where there is love, motivation, action and transformation to Christ-likeness.

Prayer

Heavenly Father, lead me to a church that is grounded in Your Word and lead me to a small group that will help in my spiritual journey of growing in Christ-likeness.

A HOUSHOLD OF FAITH

Colossians 3:13 *"Bear with one another and if one has a complaint against each other, forgive each other , as the lord has forgiven you. so you must also forgive".*

Colossians 3: 21 *"Fathers, do not embitter your children, or they will become discouraged."*

Proverbs 17:6 *"Children's children are a crown to the aged, and parents are a pride of their children".*

How do we build a household of faith?

I came to love the gospel song that was sung by Steve Green entitled *Household of Faith.* The lyrics truly resonates in my heart with it's wonderful melody and its lyrics:

"We'll build a household of faith,
that together we can make,
and when the strong winds blow, it won't fall down
as one in Him we 'll grow and the whole world will know
we are a household of faith."

Patrick and I have been married for over 30 years and have had the privilege of raising two wonderful boys.

It wasn't a breeze to raise two energetic boys. In fact it was *arduous.* Scores of patience and endurance were needed and most often, these are the moments when I was tried the most.

During our faith journey, we have been taught divine lessons from God.

Oftentimes, these divine lessons included pruning and stripping of pride, anger, weeds of anger. And with that came sicknesses, sleepless nights, physical pain.

My poor energetic boys also were the brunt of my anger and frustration at times, but I always stopped to consider the legacy I wanted to leave for my kids.

I would however, read bible stories to them and we would pray together as a family.

One of my sons was married in May 2019. Part of the program was a time when the parents of the bride and groom were honored by their children.

My son told me the impact of reading Bible stories to them when they were young. He carries that with him until the present, in his ministry.

Sometimes we think that the things we do don't have any effect on our kids, when they do and so do our attitudes in the home.

During those times when problems arose in our marriage and in our children, we have held onto God's promises and we kept praying for God to help us in our problems and to change our hearts.

Christ has become our Chief cornerstone. Prayer and God's Word have become our anchor.

I am so grateful that God sent to us a missionary couple who guided us through our journey of transformation. The transforming power of God is able to penetrate.

Building a Christian home turned out to be not so heavy a burden, but a wonderful blessing and joy. Children are very perceptive. Our hearts are laid bare before them such as our reactions to situations, our attitudes in the home, how we discuss things, and the words we say.

They can see if we are authentic, or hypocrites.

Children see when their dad is harsh to their mother and they know whether their parents put on another face in front of the church.

They simply know. They are like sponges and they are our gauge whether we truly walk the talk.

As we read Colossians, Paul, the writer , focuses on Christian living with a clear understanding that it comes from the truth of God's word.

Our identity comes from Jesus Christ so the goal is Christ-likeness – in our lives, worship and service.

There is a true transforming power by the Holy Spirit in the mind and heart of a believer, that can turn a heart of stone into a heart of flesh, a soft heart.

God has designed the family as a unit, to be one that is aligned to the will and purposes of God, a unit that will glorify Him, be a light to others who will be drawn to Him by our love for one another and obedience to God.

Marriage of one woman to one man (monogamous, and heterosexual union, as seen in 1 Corinthians 7:2), submission of the wife to the husband and the husband loving his wife (Col. 3:18-19), bible devotions as a family – these are all designed by God.

Questions to Ponder:

What is your family life like? Do you honor God with your forbearance, mercy, and tender heartedness? What legacy do you want to leave the next generation? Do you set aside time for family bible devotions and prayer?

May our authentic Christ-like attitudes be an example to our children as others may be drawn to God.

Prayer

Heavenly Father, teach us to be authentic Christ followers to lead our children to be drawn to you and leave a legacy that resonates in them to love you and follow in our footsteps.

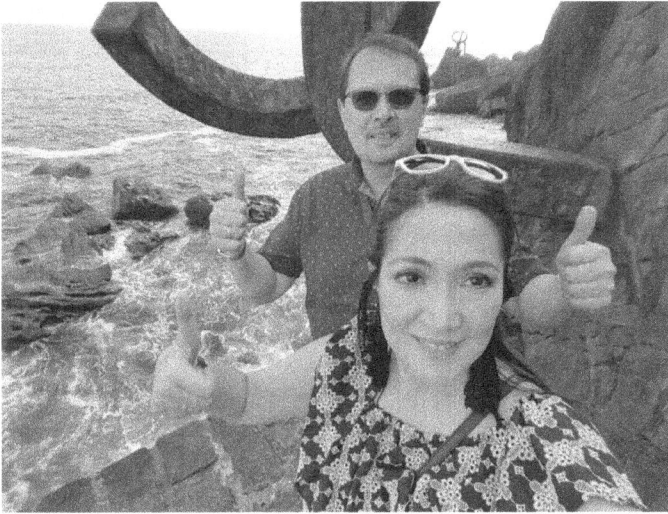

Leni with her husband Patrick in San Sebastian, Spain.

LENI HUFANA-DEL PRADO

Leni del Prado's passion lies in coaching, counselling and mentoring women and young people, so does her service to God and people from all walks of life.

Her wisdom and practical knowledge come from her introspective experience, exposure to different cultures, and interacting with people from all walks of life. She is a mentor to women, and though she wasn't trained in life coaching, some women gave her that title, as a personal life coach to them.

She and her Husband were restaurateurs at one point in their lives as they share the same love for culinary and travelling.

A graduate of The University of the Philippines, and a former title holder and first runner up of the Miss Philippines, she was ushered into a world of fashion modeling on the ramp and television commercials. She also acted and guested in television shows during her younger years.

Now, at 57 years old, she has been married for 31 years to Patrick F. del Prado. She now enjoys being a grandmother and is a proud mother of two grown men.

CHAPTER 4

DIVINELY DESIGNED RELATIONSHIPS

By Patrick Del Prado

DESTINED TO SUBMIT

J esus is Lord" is a phrase one normally hears from people who profess to be Christians.

Aside from this, we often hear expressions like "Praise the Lord!" or "The Lord reigns!" or "All glory to the Lord."

But what does calling Jesus as "Lord" really mean?

Why is it important for mankind to acknowledge Jesus as Lord?

And how should the Lordship of Christ be manifested in our lives?

These questions impact the way we live our lives today as well as our eternal destinies as outlined in the Bible.

Jesus is Lord

While Jesus was fulfilling His earthly ministry of teaching God's Word, healing the sick, and bringing joy and light to those who lived in despair, He was already called "Lord" by His disciples.

Generally speaking, a lord is someone with authority, control, or power over others. To say that someone is lord is to recognize *that* person as master or ruler of some kind. That person is in a position of preeminence in your life.

Jesus was being called "Lord" by his disciples since He was a person in authority, one who was knowledgeable about the things of God.

Those who closely followed Jesus also witnessed His authority over nature as He calmed the storm and healed the sick.

Jesus also had authority over demons. Evidence of this reality was seen in the way demons who possessed people shuddered at the presence of Jesus and immediately obeyed His commands for them to depart from people whom they were tormenting.

In Matthew 8:2 we also see the leper call Jesus "Lord", because he was showing Jesus respect as a healer and teacher.

However, after the resurrection, the title "Lord," as applied to Jesus, became much more than a title of honor or respect.

Saying, "Jesus is Lord," became a way of declaring Jesus' deity. It became an acknowledgement that Jesus is God!

In John 20:28 we read of Thomas, the one who initially doubted Jesus' resurrection, saying *"My Lord and my God!"*

The apostle Peter also had a number of pronouncements about Jesus. In Acts 2:36 we see Peter delivering his first sermon on the day of Pentecost. He declared to all the thousands present that *"God made this Jesus, whom you crucified, both Lord and Messiah."*

Later in Acts 10:36 as Peter ministered to Cornelius, the first Gentile to accept Jesus as Lord, Peter declared that Jesus is *"Lord of all."* He was in fact telling them that Jesus was both God and Savior.

Why was Peter declaring this?

In Isaiah 43:11 God asserts, *"I, even I, am the Lord, And there is no savior besides Me."* This verse only affirms Jesus as God in the flesh. Otherwise, He would not be the Savior of mankind.

Why should you declare Jesus as Lord?

This acknowledgement of Jesus as Lord is in fact linked to our salvation.

The Apostle Paul teaches in Romans 10:9-10, *"that if you confess with your mouth Jesus as Lord and believe in your heart that God raised Him from the dead, you will be saved; for with the heart a person believes, resulting in righteousness, and with the mouth he confesses, resulting in salvation."*

From this passage, we understand that it all starts with a declaration of what you believe in your heart to be true.

It starts with believing Jesus is indeed God for He has risen from the dead. Death could not hold Him and had no dominion over Him.

So is it really as easy as simply saying, "Jesus is Lord" and then you are saved? Is that *all* it takes to be saved?

I remember my own story of coming to know Jesus.

My wife and I were living in the Philippines then. The fact is I wasn't really seeking the Lord. I was content with how I was going to church every Sunday, not doing anything "bad" and thought that I was being a good Christian.

It was my wife who was more involved in the church and unbeknown to me, she was praying for my salvation.

One evening, the church she was attending, had some visiting missionaries from the U.S. and they came to visit us.

At first, I didn't want to entertain them because I was not informed beforehand that they were coming. My wife begged me to meet them and so I thought I'd be polite, say hello, then excuse myself.

I was unaware of the plans God had for me that evening.

As the missionary started sharing the Word of God, I felt drawn to the gospel message he was proclaiming. That same evening, I asked forgiveness for my past sins and prayed to accept Jesus as Lord and Savior of my life.

The missionary assured me that by my acknowledging Jesus as Lord I was now saved. I was so *overcome* with emotions then, that I simply accepted what he said.

In the days that followed, I dug into the Bible to get assurance that I was indeed saved.

You see, I had led a rebellious and sinful life for several years before I settled down and got married.

It was because of my checkered past, that I was seeking to find answers. I had done some horrible things that I was ashamed of.

Could God *really* wipe my slate clean *just* like that?

Wasn't there anything else that I could do?

I would spend hours pouring through scriptures every night. There was so much I didn't know about the Bible. There was so much that I was unaware of, about God's plan for the salvation of mankind. I was like a sponge absorbing all the teachings from God's Word.

It then became *very* clear to me that salvation was through Christ *alone* and by His grace *alone*.

In Acts 4:12, the Bible is very clear that *".. there is salvation in no one else; for there is no other name under heaven that has been given among men by which we must be saved."*

That "name" refers to none other than the Lord Jesus Christ.

Then Ephesians 2:8-9 teaches that, *"For by grace you have been saved through faith; and that not of yourselves, it is the gift of God; not as a result of works, so that no one may boast."*

What a momentous time – I was *finally* at peace. God's Word revealed and continues to reveal that I am truly 100% saved!

In my journey as a new believer, I understood that I was drawn to the message of the gospel because I saw myself as a sinner.

But that was not me at all.

It was God who unveiled my eyes to see that I could do nothing by myself to be made right with Him. I needed a Savior. This awareness enabled me to repent, forsake my sins and acknowledge Jesus as Lord and Savior of my life.

So, when you say Jesus is Lord, you have to understand that this means acknowledging Him as God who has *preeminence* in your life. This means He is in a position of absolute authority and control over your life.

Jesus Himself said in Matthew 28:18 *"All authority has been given to Me in heaven and on earth."* All your desires, thoughts, actions should be subservient to the will of Jesus for your life. He becomes your "boss" or master. It is no longer you who calls the shots, but Jesus.

Giving Up Control

The *biggest* struggle people have about submitting to Jesus as Lord is the fact that you *do* have to give up control of your life.

People have no issues believing in Jesus Christ as Lord, but it is the response to this fact that is the issue.

We all want to have a certain control over our lives. We want to have control of choices we make. If you look at though, the control we think we currently have in our life is merely an *illusion*.

The fact is – we have *zero* control! If we did, we would be able to control our future or the consequences of our choices.

The reality is, *every* aspect of our lives is actually in the hands of the almighty. He controls all things being a sovereign and omnipotent God.

So why should we cling to the *illusion* of controlling our lives when we wield *no* real power? Wouldn't it be wiser to turn our lives over, to the one who knows the very number of hairs on our head and who *genuinely* cares for us?

I have been serving as an Elder of an Evangelical church in the Philippines for over 15 years. I have seen people "fall" in their walk with the Lord more times than I wish to remember.

It deeply pains Elders and Pastors of any church to see people fall because of sin in their lives.

I have sadly encountered many people leading double lives, dabbling in the things of God and then caught up in sin when no one is watching.

That said, it is always encouraging to see people realize that they have failed God, repent, and return to living for the Lord.

These are the times when you see the powerful work of the Holy Spirit convicting the hearts of erring believers.

However, I have seen people fall and never come back. Their lives unravel and they choose to leave the church and continue living in sin. It has been heartbreaking to see people fall into adultery, lust, pornography, lying, cheating, and corruption.

Unfortunately, these decisions to continue to live in sin have devastating consequences on their families. These things have not only happened to regular members but also to Elders and people in ministry…it is heart-wrenching!

The lesson is that anyone can fall.

If we allow the world's values and worldly thinking to control any part of our lives, then we are doomed. Falling into sin and reaping its consequences is just a matter of time.

Destined to Submit

We should emulate the attitude of the apostle Paul in Galatians 2:20 when he said, *"I have been crucified with Christ; and it is no longer I who live, but Christ lives in me; and the life which I now live in the flesh I live by faith in the Son of God, who loved me and gave Himself up for me."*

It is the very mercies of God that should be your motivation to surrender your life to Him. Without Jesus, you would still be a slave to sin and be subject the wrath of God.

Yet Jesus' sacrifice on the cross fully satisfied the penalty for your sins and that of every person. We have been redeemed and now our lives no longer belong to us.

1 Corinthians 6:20 reminds us, *"For you have been bought with a price: therefore glorify God in your body."* This denotes fully surrendering the way we live to God's will, as expressed in the Bible.

In Philippians 2:9-11 we are told, *"For this reason also, God highly exalted Him, and bestowed on Him the name which is above every name, so that at the name of Jesus every knee will bow, of those who are in heaven and on earth and under the earth, and that every tongue will confess that Jesus Christ is Lord, to the glory of God the Father."*

So you see we are ALL destined to submit to Jesus as Lord.

This verse tells us *"every knee will bow"* and *"every tongue confess that Jesus is Lord."* This means *no one* regardless of belief or creed, *will be exempted.*

It is God's will that Jesus is glorified and magnified as Lord of all. Jesus as Lord of all is a fact whether people acknowledge this or not. It doesn't diminish this from being true and certainly doesn't diminish the glory that already belongs to the Lord Jesus.

The question is, will *you* submit to Jesus as Lord – willingly and happily now, or grudgingly and painfully during the time of judgement?

A.W. Tozer once said *"Christ will be Lord or He will be Judge. Every man must decide whether to take Him as Lord now or face Him as Judge then."*

Jesus as TRUE Lord of your Life

This is such a critical topic that we all need to take to heart, because our eternal destiny is at stake.

It is important to understand the weight, gravity, and responsibility of declaring Jesus is Lord of your life.

The word "Lord" is not something we use loosely but rather with reverence.

Sadly, even to those who profess to be Christians, Jesus is not truly Lord of their lives. This is not meant to pass judgement on anyone, but this conclusion comes from the very words of the Lord Jesus Himself.

In Matthew 7:21-23, Jesus says, *"Not everyone who says to Me, 'Lord, Lord,' will enter the kingdom of heaven, but he who does the will of My Father who is in heaven will enter. Many will say to Me on that day, 'Lord, Lord, did we not prophesy in Your name, and in Your name cast out demons, and in Your name perform many miracles?' And then I will declare to them, 'I never knew you; depart from Me, you who practice lawlessness.'"*

The verses tell us that merely calling Jesus "Lord" is *not* a guarantee that we are true followers. It is *not* a matter of believing in our heads that Jesus is Lord for even demons believe in Jesus and yet they are *not* saved.

We can also glean from the verses that those who were calling Him, "Lord, Lord" where people in ministry – those who were active in the things of God. They were busy doing things that we attribute to Christians, even strong or mature Christians.

Yet, the Lord says, *"I never knew you; depart from Me, you who practice lawlessness."*

This would be the most miserable words to hear and the greatest rejection coming from someone you thought you were serving! Worse is the declaration that *you* are practicing lawlessness!

There is a *huge* difference with those who merely say "Jesus is Lord" vs. those who really install Jesus as the Lord of their lives. The difference lies in our obedience and submission to the Lord Jesus.

In saying, "Jesus is Lord," we commit ourselves to *obey* Him.

In Luke 6:46 Jesus asked, *"Why do you call me, 'Lord, Lord,' and do not do what I say?"* An acknowledgement of Jesus' Lordship is logically accompanied by a *submission* to Jesus' authority.

If Jesus is Lord, then He owns us; He has the right to tell us what to do.

His lordship doesn't merely apply to *some* things in our lives but *every* aspect of our life.

The Lord doesn't want 95% or 97% of our lives but 100% of our lives!

When we ask the Lord to come in and reign in our hearts, it should be an invitation to reign in *every* room or chamber.

Nothing is off limits. Nothing we are still clinging on to and unwilling to surrender to the Lord Jesus is off limits to His Holy Spirit.

A person who says, "Jesus is Lord," with a full understanding of what that means, i.e. that Jesus is God and has supreme authority over all things – has been divinely enlightened.

In 1 Corinthians 12:3 we are told that *"…no one can say, 'Jesus is Lord,' except by the Holy Spirit."*

It has been said that the Christian life is *not* difficult but *impossible.*

We cannot begin to understand, let alone *live out* the commands of God, without the enlightenment and empowerment from the Holy Spirit.

It is the Holy Spirit who unveils our eyes to see our true condition before God. It is the Holy Spirit who gives us the faith to understand and respond to the gospel. It is also the Holy Spirit who empowers us to surrender our lives moment by moment to the Lord.

Every thought, every word, every action, all in alignment to God's purposes. Then our life becomes a reflection of honoring God by the choices we make.

If you don't have the Holy Spirit actively working in your life, you have to consider whether or not you are a true believer.

In Acts 2:38 Peter tells us, *"Repent, and each of you be baptized in the name of Jesus Christ for the forgiveness of your sins; and you will receive the gift of the Holy Spirit."* There must be *genuine* repentance and submission to the Lord before the Holy Spirit indwells us.

To sum up the idea of the Lordship of Christ, it does not consist of one act of obedience but rather is measured by the sum of our obedience. And it cannot be accomplished in our own strength or power, but by the power available to us by the indwelling Holy Spirit.

We are strongest when we are relying on Him.

Evidence of Submission

There are generally three areas where the submission to the Lordship of Jesus is seen in our lives: **TIME**, **TREASURE**, and **TALENTS**.

1. TIME

We all have been given the same amount each day.

24 hours or 1,440 minutes. That's it.

We *cannot* carry over the time we did not use to the next day.

There is *no* going back in time as well. What we decide to do with our time will determine whether we are being drawn closer or farther from the Lord.

We are stewards of this precious gift that most people take for granted.

And whether we agree with it or not, *what* we do with our time reflects what is *truly* important to us.

In Philippians 3:13-14 (NASB), the apostle Paul likens the Christian walk to a race. *"Brethren, I do not regard myself as having laid hold of it yet; but one thing I do: forgetting what lies behind and reaching forward to what lies ahead, I press on toward the goal for the prize of the upward call of God in Christ Jesus. Let us therefore, as many as are perfect, have this attitude; and if in anything you have a different attitude, God will reveal that also to you; however, let us keep living by that same standard to which we have attained."*

The proper use of our time starts with the right attitude.

These verses are from the Apostle Paul who has been credited with writing a *major portion* of the New Testament and whose teaching constitutes a lot of Christian doctrine.

Yet, look at his attitude. His humility is *inspiring* at the same time *convicting.*

First, he didn't see himself yet as having laid hold of being all he could be for Jesus. Because of this attitude, he *didn't* rely on his past successes in winning people for the Lord, or his overcoming numerous trials and persecution as reasons to slow down in his fervor for the Lord.

Instead, he "presses on", which reflects a continuous striving to become more Christ-like in everything he did.

He did not view the Christian life as a sprint, but rather a marathon. As such, he didn't only want to *start* strong but to also run strong, and to *finish* strong.

If this is the attitude of Paul, how do you think his typical day would look like? How much time would he have spent meditating on God's Word, in prayer and sitting at the feet of Jesus?

In 1 Corinthians 9:27 he says, *"but I discipline my body and make it my slave, so that, after I have preached to others, I myself will not be disqualified."*

He is very intentional about ensuring that he disciplines his body – his thoughts, words, and actions toward things that are godly and that help strengthen him in his Christian walk.

Make no mistake. This is *not* about Paul having strong willpower. It is about Paul *choosing* to obey and then *relying* on the Holy Spirit to give him strength.

What does this all mean to you and me today?

Having been in this earth for 58 years, my thoughts are now focused on how I should live out the last chapter of my life. I, too, want to finish strong *for* the Lord and *in* the Lord.

Yet we live in a world *full* of constant distractions where so many things compete for our time and attention. Aside from traditional time we allot for family and work, we also have time allotted for social media, networking, sports, Netflix, and self-improvement.

How do we manage these competing priorities? Does the example of Paul still apply in this day and age?

It may be a worthwhile exercise to think about how you spend your time today.

Pull out a piece of paper and list down the activities that are part of your typical day.

Assign percentages to the buckets of activities where you spend your time today.

It is only after you accomplish this exercise that you will understand what is *truly* important to you. It will also explain the state you are in with your life.

Are you happy with what you discovered?

How much time are you spending reading the Bible? How often do you pray each day? Are you satisfied with remembering the Lord only in short prayers before meals? Are you allocating any time to commune with the Lord?

In John 15:5, the Lord tells us, *"I am the vine, you are the branches; he who abides in Me and I in him, he bears much fruit, for apart from Me you can do nothing."*

How then do we abide in the One we do not really know in an intimate way? It follows therefore, that if we are not bearing fruit in our Christian walk that we have not been *truly* connected to the vine. Our lives are *deprived* of the nourishment it desperately needs from the Lord.

If we want to change the current state of our lives to reflect our submission to the Lord, we must be intentional about prioritizing our time with what is truly important.

If Jesus is Lord, He deserves our time and attention.

We must spend time seeking and understanding His will, purpose, and commands for us. We must carve out *more* time for God and *less* time for social media, TV, or other things that do not cause us to be stronger in our Christian walk.

Ephesians 5:15-16 warns us, *"Therefore be careful how you walk, not as unwise men but as wise, making the most of your time, because the days are evil."*

2. TREASURE

A key area that reflects how much we have yielded to the Lordship of Jesus is confirmed by how much we have surrendered our wallets to Him.

We *cannot* truly say that Jesus is our Lord if we are still acting like lords of our finances.

Our heavenly Father owns it all! Everything we possess actually belongs to God and He has made us temporary stewards.

We do not leave our money behind when we die; we leave God's money.

He has unlimited resources to meet each one of our needs at His disposal. However, He is also a good Father who gives us what we need in His perfect timing and He grants our desires according to His will.

As children of God, we have the responsibility to trust in Him with all our hearts regarding money, despite our circumstances.

My intention is not to be legalistic about the percentage of your income that should go to the coffers of the church you belong.

The more important aspect of surrendering our finances is the peace and blessing we receive from being *obedient* and trusting the Lord. We cannot out-give the Creator of the universe who is sovereign above all created beings.

In the Old Testament, the people of God were commanded to tithe. It was always intended as a way of honoring God with the blessing He had bestowed.

Yet, many disobeyed and God likened this to robbing Him.

In Malachi 3:10 God commands, *"Bring the whole tithe into the storehouse, so that there may be food in My house, and test Me now in this,"* says the Lord of hosts, *"if I will not open for you the windows of heaven and pour out for you a blessing until it overflows."*

The Bible does warn us against testing God, yet here God tells us to "test Him" regarding His faithfulness to those who *entrust their finances* to Him.

In the New Testament the Lord again reiterates His command and promise.

In Luke 6:38 it says, *"Give, and it will be given to you. They will pour into your lap a good measure—pressed down, shaken together, and running over. For by your standard of measure it will be measured to you in return."*

If you are not entrusting God with your finances, you are unknowingly entrusting this to something else.

Maybe it is a house you are saving for, or a car, or your child's education. These may be good goals.

But if you hold back from giving back to the Lord, you are in fact saying that you do not trust the Lord to bless you. You do not trust His promises outlined in scriptures. You are in effect saying that for your goals to materialize, it is up to you and not up to God.

This mindset is ignoring the fact that God is sovereign. The danger with this way of thinking is that God may take away whatever is becoming your source of confidence.

Our reluctance to give back faithfully to God may be the *biggest* hindrance to living victoriously for the Lord. The Lord *cannot* mightily use one who is still very attached to the things of the world.

Jesus declares in Matthew 6:24 *"No one can serve two masters; for either he will hate the one and love the other, or he will be devoted to one and despise the other. You cannot serve God and wealth."*

In making the choice, *do* take note that it is a choice between the *temporal* and the *eternal*.

The area of surrendering my finances was one of my struggles early in my journey as a believer.

Having been raised a Catholic, I saw from my childhood the amount of money given by people in church. I also served as an altar boy for a while early in my high school years.

One of my tasks was to count the money in the offering bag and hand this over to the Parish Priest. People would generally just give loose change in their pockets and if there were paper bills, these were not large amounts. This is why I struggled with the idea of giving generously at first. But the Lord worked in my heart to trust in Him and not the works of my hands.

Now, one of the *biggest* joys in my Christian walk is to be able to give back to God what is His and bless others with what He has blessed me with.

3. TALENTS

Just as we have been entrusted with time and money, God has also entrusted each one of us with certain talents and Spiritual gifts.

We are likewise stewards of these talents and Spiritual gifts that we should use according to God's design and desire.

Unfortunately, many Christians go to work with the idea that their talents are to be used *solely* for their own benefit.

We have to realize that God gave us talents to benefit others also, not only ourselves.

And God has likewise blessed other people with talents that are meant to benefit you.

There are certain principles we have to be cognizant of, to become good stewards of the talents and Spiritual gifts we have been given:

- *We are blessed to bless others* – If you are good with carpentry, car engines, technology, music, or arts and crafts, those talents or abilities are not given to you for the sole purpose of your enjoyment or to make money with. These were given so that you may be a source of blessing to others and that God may be praised and glorified. If you have these gifts, start looking for ways to honor God by using your talents to help others.

In 1 Peter 4:10 we are told, *"As each one has received a special gift, employ it in serving one another as good stewards of the manifold grace of God."*

Though this verse refers to the exercise of spiritual gifts within the church, the principle of being a blessing to others carries over to talents. So, try to seek out those who may need or could use your talents and abilities. Start with your church first then move on to helping people you know or maybe even blessing others in your community.

- **We are to bring glory to God** – we are all uniquely made and uniquely gifted by the Lord. Each one is blessed with spiritual gifts and talents to bring glory to God.

This fact is confirmed by the apostle Paul in 1 Corinthians 7:7 when he said, *"Yet I wish that all men were even as I myself am. However, each man has his own gift from God, one in this manner, and another in that."*

What is the difference between talents and gifts? Talents are natural while gifts are supernatural. Talents are natural endowments received at birth, although some talents can be honed in life. Gifts on the other hand are received at the time of your new birth after receiving Jesus as Lord and Savior. Talents are possessed by both believers and unbelievers.

In 1 Peter 4:10-11 believers are encouraged, *"As each has received a gift, use it to serve one another, as good stewards of God's varied grace: whoever speaks, as one who speaks oracles of God; whoever serves, as one who serves by the strength that God supplies—in order that in everything God may be glorified."*

It is clear that Spiritual gifts are imparted to us, and then to be imparted to others, for building the body of Christ. Each of us is given different gifts, all used to serve by various ministries and needs of the church.

The Lord has given believers in every church all the Spiritual gifts to allow them to thrive.

The issue lies with believers choosing to use their gifts and their talents for the Lord. This again is where the question of surrendering all of ourselves to the Lord comes into play.

It is my prayer that through this message you have gained a clear understanding of what it means to declare Jesus as Lord.

We are all destined to submit to the Lord because this is the will of God. The Lord is pleased when we do so willingly and as a rightful response to a loving God.

What is so encouraging is that as we surrender every facet of our lives to the Lord, He empowers us to live victorious Christian lives.

We realize and experience that God's plan for our lives is so much better than any plan we can think of.

We are also called to wholeheartedly submit our *time*, *treasure*, and *talents* to the Lord – for He alone is worthy of everything we have and everything we are.

Submitting is a privilege and a joy for a believer.

Why?

Because He is the Savior of our souls – our Lord to whom all glory belongs!

Worship Him Who is Worthy, Harden Not Your Heart

We are living in unprecedented times.

Covid-19 has put the world on lockdown and many lives are on pause.

It is a time when even the high and mighty have to adhere to restrictions on movement and observance of health protocols.

No doubt, the situation has caused inconvenience and suffering all over the world. We see a lot of frustration and desperation among people especially those who have lost their means of livelihood.

There is so much anxiety and fear *in* the air.

People are starting to wonder why this is happening? Why now? Why us?

It is difficult to answer why God allowed this pandemic to happen and I won't attempt to do so.

God in His divine wisdom has a purpose for all this – a purpose for the world and a purpose for you.

One thing I believe is true though, is that *this* is a wakeup call for *all* of us.

It is time to take stock of what is truly important and what should take priority in our lives. We are being given the opportunity by God to seriously consider what has eternal value, and then reshaping our priorities accordingly.

While many countries are making plans to slowly open up, the threat of Covid 19 will be here for months, perhaps years.

Masks and social distancing will be the new normal. There will still be many fears and anxieties that linger in people's minds. There is so much uncertainty on what the future will look like. No one can say for sure.

Even the wealthiest of nations don't have the answer.

We have all been impacted by Covid 19 in different ways.

For some, the job security they used to enjoy is now at risk. Worse, others may lose their jobs completely as companies and businesses struggle to stay afloat.

Then we have all the travel restrictions that prevent us from visiting family members and loved ones who are also contending with quarantine restrictions.

It is with this backdrop of fear, anxieties, and uncertainty that I share this message – which is an invitation to worship and also a warning against *unbelief*. Psalm 95 is a wonderful psalm that reminds us to focus our attention and affection constantly toward God regardless of the situation we're in.

> Psalm 95: *"1 O come, let us sing for joy to the Lord, Let us shout joyfully to the Rock of our salvation. 2 Let us come before His presence with thanksgiving, Let us shout joyfully to Him with psalms.3 For the Lord is a great God And a great King above all gods, 4 In whose hand are the depths of the earth, The peaks of the mountains are His also.5 The sea is His, for it was He who made it, And His hands formed the dry land. 6 Come, let us worship and bow down,*
> *Let us kneel before the Lord our Maker. 7 For He is our God, And we are the people of His pasture and the sheep of His hand. Today, if you would hear His voice, 8 Do not harden your hearts, as at Meribah, As in the day of Massah in the wilderness, 9 "When your fathers tested Me, They tried Me, though they had seen My work. 10 "For forty years I loathed that generation, And said they are a people who err in their heart, And they do not know My ways.11 "Therefore I swore in My anger, Truly they shall not enter into My rest."*

We have 11 very insightful verses that I will aim to unpack by dividing the devotion into **5 sections** using the following outline:

i) Worship as people of God;
ii) He is worthy of our worship;
iii) Worship Him humbly;

Then the last 2 sections give us warnings:

i) Do not harden your heart; and
ii) Do not grieve the Lord.

i) Worship as People of God

Let us start with the invitation for all believers to worship God in Psalm 95:1-2 – *"1 O come, let us sing for joy to the Lord, Let us shout joyfully to the rock of our salvation. 2 Let us come before His presence with thanksgiving, Let us shout joyfully to Him with psalms."*

In these verses we, as believers are called to sing for joy for the Lord.

Note that on three occasions it says *"let us,"* meaning we worship God with songs as a community or as a fellowship of believers.

While singing is not the only way we are to worship, we can see throughout that Scripture calls us to worship through singing. Songs are the emotional expression of what is in our hearts.

While others around us may hear the words of the songs we are singing, we are not singing for them. We must remember that the object of our worship is the Lord. He sees our hearts and knows whether our thoughts wander as we sing or if we are focused on honoring Him.

So, whether we are singing together in person or virtually as a fellowship, we should do so in the moment, sincerely and fervently.

If we take a critical look at the way we view or even participate in singing songs of worship in a church service, I am sure many will not consider it as important as the sermon or the observance of the Lord's supper.

I have had the privilege of attending church services in a number of countries and I see the same thing. There are those who are enthusiastically singing, and there are those who are simply standing quietly, waiting for this part of the service to end.

Honestly, I too, on occasion have found my mind drifting off to other things while the singing in church was going on. I would start thinking about where to take my family for lunch after the service ends, or sometimes I think about work.

There is definitely a lot of room to improve on, in this area of worship.

Psalm 100:1 (KJV) says *"Make a joyful noise unto the Lord..."*

What *is* a joyful noise?

A joyful noise begins with a pure heart wanting to praise God.

When we are filled with the Holy Spirit, we desire to sing to Him and edify others around us.

Musical talent has *nothing* to do with it. This should be an encouragement to those who don't consider themselves as singers.

You see, it is *not* the voice quality that matters but the *intent* of our hearts. When the focus of our hearts is God and His greatness, our noise is a sweet sound to His ears.

Verse 1 of Psalm 95 also tells us to *"shout joyfully to the Rock of our salvation."* "Shouting" here is *not* about screaming, but refers to an *unashamed enthusiasm* toward God as our refuge and rescuer.

It is God who protects us from physical harm and sickness. This is very evident during the time of this writing, with Covid 19 having global impact.

How long has this virus been wreaking havoc? How long has God been protecting you and your family?

Sometimes we pay too much attention on the lockdown and the inconvenience of being cooped up in our homes for long periods of time, that we forget to praise God for His protection. We take it for granted.

And not only for our protection but also the way He is protecting our loved ones wherever they may be in the world.

And our Lord being the Rock of our salvation goes *beyond* the physical realm. Jesus provides us the ultimate spiritual deliverance with His finished work of the cross. He is the Rock of our salvation, a sure and eternal Refuge for us.

In verse 2 we are told *"2 Let us come before His presence with thanksgiving, Let us shout joyfully to Him with psalms."* The original intent of this invitation was not for the Jews to come into the Holy of Holies in the tabernacle, but rather come into the *spiritual* presence of God.

This is also the application for us today. We, as people of God – do not sing to an empty space. He is in our midst and we are in His presence. There is true connection between God and His people in a time of worship.

Our worship must express a heart of thanksgiving to our God who has done so much for us.

In Psalm 69:30 David declares *"I will praise the name of God with song And magnify Him with thanksgiving."*

It is a good practice to regularly reflect on the blessings of the Lord regardless of our current reality – whether we are in a season of plenty, or a season of want or trials.

As we intentionally reflect on the Lord's blessings, we will be reminded that everything around us, in experiences we have throughout the day, there will always be a reason to praise the Lord. For example, we often overlook the fact that every single breath we take is a blessing for the Lord.

My first mentor when I was young in the Christian faith had a great practice worthy of emulating. He and his family maintained a "Book of Remembrance" where they recorded all of God's blessings and answered prayers.

So in times when they were weighed down with the problems in life, they would open the pages and be encouraged by the history of God's faithfulness.

He is a God who blesses and oftentimes the problems we face are the blessings themselves. Because it is in times of problems that we are brought to our knees and refocus on the Lord. We become sensitive to His leading and become attentive to His convictions.

I like this familiar quote from Rick Warren that is worth mentioning, *"In happy moments, praise God. In difficult moments, seek God. In quiet moments, worship God. In painful moments, trust God. Every moment, thank God."*

Psalm 98:4 also encourages us to *"shout joyfully to the Lord…sing praises."*

The Book of Psalms is a collection of songs of worship and also a book of prayer and praise. Many of the songs we sing today are pulled out from the book of Psalms.

From the psalms we see words of worship that verbalize God's worth to us. There are also words of praise that shine the light on God's faithfulness in our lives.

Then there are words of prayer expressing the deepest longings of the psalmists to God our Creator.

What is most encouraging to me in the Book of Psalms is the honesty of the writers in expressing their feelings to the Lord. Yes, you see the sincerity in their praise for the Lord, and also their honesty in expressing their fears and frustrations to the Almighty.

ii) He is Worthy of our Worship

In Psalm 95:3-5 we read *"3 For the Lord is a great God and a great King above all gods,4 In whose hand are the depths of the earth, The peaks of the mountains are His also. 5 The sea is His, for it was He who made it, And His hands formed the dry land."*

Why do we worship our God?

It I because the Lord is a GREAT God!

Fully understanding the greatness of our God helps us to properly worship Him. We should never lose our awe of who God is.

Awe is defined as a *"feeling of reverential respect mixed with fear or wonder."*

What then does it mean to be in awe of God?

To understand what we are to be in awe of, let us read Romans 11:33 *"33 Oh, the depth of the riches both of the wisdom and knowledge of God! How unsearchable are His judgments and unfathomable His ways!"*

This verse reminds us why we should look to God in awe every day of our lives.

God is so *beyond* our understanding, and we will never be able to search out all the wonders of His ways, His judgements, His riches, His wisdom, and His knowledge. The greatness and majesty of God are *far* beyond our comprehension!

There is a risk for prayer, worship, and bible reading to become routine in a believer's life to the point that these become *"tick the box"* activities.

To avoid this, we should never lose our sense of awe of God – to be constantly overwhelmed with wonder at the depth of the greatness of God.

Verse 3 also declares that *"God is a great King above all gods."*

Charles Spurgeon in his commentary about this verse wrote: *"No doubt the surrounding nations imagined Jehovah to be merely a local deity, the god of a small nation and therefore one of the inferior deities, the psalmist utterly repudiates such an idea."*

When we compare other gods to the Lord, we can see how bankrupt they are in majesty and power to God as Creator.

That truth is reinforced in Psalm 96:4-5 *"4 For great is the Lord and greatly to be praised; He is to be feared above all gods.5 For all the gods of the peoples are idols, But the Lord made the heavens."*

As we go back to verses 4 & 5 of Psalm 95 we read, *"4 In whose hand are the depths of the earth, The peaks of the mountains are His also. 5 The sea is His, for it was He who made it, And His hands formed the dry land."*

The best way God's greatness is displayed is by His mastery over creation.

From the lowest valley to the highest mountains; from the sea to the dry land, God's hands formed them. The oceans and the seas of this world belong to God. Nations may stake their claim on the South China Sea, but the psalmist makes clear that *"the sea is His."*

If God owns the seas because He made them, He owns us as well because He made us. We are His creation and therefore, our Creator has the right to have His divine will play out in our lives.

In Isaiah 40:28 we read *"28 Do you not know? Have you not heard? The Everlasting God, the Lord, the Creator of the ends of the earth Does not become weary or tired. His understanding is inscrutable."*

Our God existed before all things.

In Genesis we read that He created the heavens and the earth by speaking them into existence. He also breathed His own life into man and man became a living soul.

God is the great Designer and Architect of everything in the universe. As the sovereign God, He is not limited by our understanding nor by time, space or matter. Truly He is a GREAT God!

iii) Worship Him Humbly

It is with the understanding of how great God is, that we should worship Him humbly.

Psalm 95:6-7 reads, *"Come, let us worship and bow down, Let us kneel before the Lord our Maker. 7 For He is our God, And we are the people of His pasture and the sheep of His hand…"*

As we start to grasp the greatness of our God and how insignificant we are in comparison, it is only fitting that we come to Him in *humility* and *reverence*.

Sometimes I feel that believers forget the humility and reverence that we should bestow upon God.

Sometimes it seems that we become too casual and familiar with God as if He were our peer.

Yes, the Bible tells us that we are no longer enemies and are now His friends, but He is *still* the Almighty. We still should maintain the utmost respect when we come before His presence.

Since the original readers of this psalm were the Israelites, let us consider at how *they* viewed worship. The different Hebrew expressions of worship means bowing, kneeling, or lying prostrate on the ground before the Lord. This is done to demonstrate our humility *and* devotion to Him.

Because of His love, grace, power, and wisdom are so much greater than ours, we are naturally moved to bow down to Him.

When we think about who God is and everything He has done for us, we can only bow and even lie prostrate before Him. We owe humble worship to God because He made us.

The act of worship is an obligation that we as the created beings owe to our Creator.

And as believers who have been redeemed by the Lord Jesus, we have at least two great reasons to humbly worship God. He is both our Maker and our Redeemer! We belong to Him twice over – in *both* creation and redemption.

In verse 7 we are reminded that *"7 For He is our God, And we are the people of His pasture and the sheep of His hand."*

This verse conjures images of the Lord as our good Shepherd. We belong to Him and so He governs, feeds, protects, and even disciplines us for our own good. We are sheep under His loving care. We know His voice and we follow Him. He leads us to green pastures where we are at peace and rest in Him.

iv) Do Not Harden Your Hearts

Now we move to the warnings in Psalm 95:7-9

> *"Today, if you would hear His voice,8 Do not harden your hearts, as at Meribah, As in the day of Massah in the wilderness, 9 "When your fathers tested Me, They tried Me, though they had seen My work."*

These words of warning in verse 7-8 are important enough to be referenced three times in the book of Hebrews 3:7-8,15; and 4:7.

I would like to focus on the word *"today"* at the start of verse 7.

This indicates the urgency of listening to God with a soft heart *today*. We have no time to lose. Tomorrow may be too late. Tomorrow God may be silent.

When you hear His voice commanding you, inviting you, or encouraging you – listen and obey. Respond to God *today* – now!

The intention to obey should not be deferred until tomorrow or put off for the future.

I have met many people – men mostly, who think that they can live their lives the way they please and then turn their lives over to God when they grow old.

They want to devote the best years of their life to chasing worldly pursuits and the pleasures of life. Then they intend to give to God whatever is left over when they are in their sixties or seventies!

There is so much folly in this way of thinking.

All God's commands relate to the present.

We cannot plan on repenting or obeying or giving up worldly desires or embrace the gospel at some point in the future. We are called to listen to His voice and obey *now* – at this present time.

Verses 8-9 of Psalm 95 references the rebellion recorded in Exodus chapter 17 where the Israelites quarreled with Moses about the lack of water, and Moses rebuked the Israelites for testing Yahweh.

Exodus 17:7 states that it was on this account that the place gained the name Massah, meaning "testing", and the name Meribah (Exodus 17:7) meaning "quarreling".

These were the same Israelites who saw the power of God in delivering them from the oppression of Pharaoh. They saw God's power when He unleashed the 10 plagues that devasted Egypt, the parting of the Red Sea, and the destruction of the entire Egyptian army!

As they set off for the Promised Land they experienced God's presence with a pillar of cloud during the day to lead the way, and a pillar of fire at night to give them light.

Yet even *after* seeing and experiencing all this, they refused to trust God whenever they faced trials or difficulties like when they had no water to drink.

Instead of trusting God, they were filled with fear, unbelief, concern and grumbling.

So does this warning against *unbelief* apply to us today?

It is highly likely that we equate *unbelief* with those who don't put their faith and trust in Jesus. As such, we don't count Christians as those who could be guilty of unbelief.

But let me stress that anyone's hearts can be hardened due to *unbelief*, even faithful Christians.

The reason I say this comes from the example of the apostles themselves – those who walked closely with the Lord.

In Mark 8:17-21 we read of this story where Jesus rebukes them for their unbelief: *"17 And Jesus, aware of this, *said to them, "Why do you discuss the fact that you have no bread? Do you not yet see or understand? Do you have a hardened heart? 18 Having eyes, do you not see? And having ears, do you not hear? And do you not remember, 19 when I broke the five loaves for the five thousand, how many baskets full of broken pieces you picked up?" They *said to Him, "Twelve." 20 "When I broke the seven for the four thousand, how many large baskets full of broken pieces did you pick up?" And they *said to Him, "Seven." 21 And He was saying to them, "Do you not yet understand?"*

The apostles were concerned about the supply of bread and completely forgot that very recently Jesus had just fed four thousand with only a few loaves and a few fishes.

Before that miracle, they had also witnessed the healing of a demon-possessed man, the physical healing of various sick people, *and* a child raised back from the dead.

And in relation to the bread, they had also experienced not too long before, the feeding of the five thousand with five loaves and two fish.

They had seen the Lord's power over nature and even over the spiritual realm.

Yet here they were showing their *unbelief* by worrying that they did not have enough bread while they were in the presence of the Lord Himself.

In verse 17. the Lord rebukes *them "Why do you discuss the fact that you have no bread? Do you not yet see or understand? Do you have a hardened heart?"*

Jesus asked if their hearts were hardened – meaning unable to see, understand, hear, and remember that He is the Sovereign Lord.

In times of distress, problems, or calamities, even believers show their unbelief by quickly forgetting how faithful the Lord has been in their lives.

We tend to forget the times He's answered our prayers, protected us from harm and sickness, or answered our call for deliverance from financial problems.

Instead, we worry and fret about our current situation.

Worse, we try to find remedies to our situation *by our own strength* and not relying on God.

This is why the Lord asked His apostles and is asking us today, *"Do you not yet understand?"*

Our understanding of who God is, affects our behavior and the way we relate to Him.

Paul was one person who truly understood that his life was in the loving hands of God, so he confidently declared in Philippians 4:19 *"19 And my God will supply all your needs according to His riches in glory in Christ Jesus."*

v) Do Not Grieve the Lord

We have a final warning in Psalm 95:10-11 *"For forty years I loathed that generation, And said they are a people who err in their heart, And they do not know My ways. 11 "Therefore I swore in My anger, Truly they shall not enter into My rest."*

God offered the generation that came out of Egypt the opportunity to take the Promised Land by *faith.*

Their unbelieving rejection of God's offer grieved Him for 40 years.

Their *unbelief* was an insult to God and prompted a solemn and angry declaration from the Lord that they would *not* enter the Promised Land.

As they wandered in the wilderness, their hearts *also* wandered from the Lord and they knew *not* His ways.

Unbelief is such a constant and dangerous temptation that we must help each other overcome it. We must understand that *unbelief* – meaning not trusting and believing that He is sufficient – grieves the Lord.

Hebrews 3:14 tells us: *"14 For we have become partakers of Christ, if we hold fast the beginning of our assurance firm until the end."*

What does this mean?

This means that holding on in faith to the end should be the collective goal of God's people.

Those who persevere and continue trusting God regardless of their circumstances are able confirm that their faith is genuine. They are *not* fair weather Christians whose enthusiasm for God is dependent on their circumstances.

We have to remember that to *know* God is to *trust* Him.

We may not always see or even understand His divine purpose especially when He allows problems and even calamities in our lives.

So if the current situation with Covid19 is adversely affecting you or your family, always remember we serve a sovereign God who *is* in control.

Pastor Peter Tanchi of Christ Commission Fellowship in the Philippines often reminds the congregation, *"Do not interpret God based on your circumstances. You must interpret your circumstances based on who God is."*

In closing, while Covid 19 might be with us for longer than we would like, we must *not* take our gaze away from our God.

This is a timely reminder to worship Him who is worthy and to harden *not* your heart.

We as believers are to worship with thanksgiving and praise as people of God.

We are to do so we unashamed enthusiasm for who He is. He is a great and awesome God, worthy of our worship. We are to worship Him humbly as created beings recognizing that He as our Creator, is above all things. We must also recognize that *unbelief* is a temptation that even believers are not immune from.

As such, we ought to be careful *not* to harden our hearts and grieve the Lord.

God bless you.

MATCH MADE IN HEAVEN

Most couples who choose to get married would want their relationship to be described as "a match made in heaven." This means that the couple was perfectly suited for each other and would likely translate to a happy and successful marriage.

With the divorce rates across the world pushing close to the fifty percent mark, this only indicates that matches made in heaven are hard to find.

Why?

Because a match made in heaven starts with God who is in heaven. The coming together of a couple has to be according to the will and purpose of God for both individuals.

The marriages that end in failure often do so because they got married for the wrong reasons.

Both man and woman go into marriage with different expectations of each other. They both express their love for each other, but their individual definition of love is different.

One party looks forward to emotional intimacy while the other is looking for sexual intimacy. This is where the problem starts, festers, then unravels until both want out of the relationship.

Their marriage is characterized by endless arguments, harshness, unkind words and actions that escalate quickly to contempt for each other. Some even degenerate into violence.

We are seeing marriages end so much faster in recent years. It is likewise alarming to see very little difference in divorce rates between professing Christians and non-Christians.

Then we have marriages that remain afloat *out of obligation* to the vows the couple made to God or for the sake their children.

Sometimes they hang on for the sake of appearances for the approval of friends, family, or society.

They go through the motions of married life. Individuals not truly happy but choosing to stay married. They just go with the flow and take things as they come.

While society widely acknowledges marriages that last, it is also worthwhile to recognize the importance of *quality* over quantity. The nature of the relationship is surely more important than the number of years a couple stays together.

Is there such a thing then as "a match made in heaven"? Is it even possible?

Many couples who are seeing these very low success rates in marriage opt not to tie the knot at all.

More and more we see people comfortable and content with living together without having to get married. They claim marriage is passé and no longer relevant in this day and age.

Those who have this perspective may have come from broken families or who have close friends with failed marriages.

The problem with this thinking is it contributes to the *breakdown of morality* in this world because it is *contrary* to God's design for mankind.

As early as the creation of man, God intended that both man and woman be united in marriage.

Genesis 2:18-25 tells us:

> *"Then the Lord God said, 'It is not good for the man to be alone; I will make him a helper suitable for him.' Out of the ground the Lord God formed every beast of the field and every bird of the sky and brought them to the man to see what he would call them; and whatever the man called a living creature, that was its name. The man gave names to all the cattle, and to the birds of the sky, and to every beast of the field,* **but for Adam there was not found a helper suitable for him**. *So the Lord God caused a deep sleep to fall upon the man, and he slept; then He took one of his ribs and closed up the flesh at that place.* **The Lord God fashioned into a woman the rib which He had taken from the man** *and brought her to the man. The man said, 'This is now bone of my bones, And flesh of my flesh; She shall be called Woman, Because she was taken out of Man.' For this reason a man shall leave his father and his mother and be joined to his wife; and they shall become one flesh. And* **the man and his wife** *were both naked and were not ashamed."*

It is important to point out that God made man in His image and likeness and so He understands man's need for love, intimacy, and fellowship in life.

The design and intent of marriage was from the heart of a loving God. He instituted marriage as a sacred ordinance for his creation whom He loved. It was *not* invented by mankind. We should therefore take our cue from our Maker.

There are very important observations coming out of these verses.

First, God did not intend man to be alone and in a state of celibacy. While different religious groups may have a different say on the matter, it was never God's design for a man to go through life celibate.

Second, God made the woman out of the man, to illustrate the most intimate and closest union.

The man should always consider the woman as a part of himself. As such, the man should endeavor to love, protect, nourish, and support his wife.

A husband is in fact commanded in Ephesians 5:33 to *"love his own wife even as himself, and the wife must see to it that she respects her husband."*

Third, God made the woman to be a wife, companion, and helper of man. *"You complete me"* – a famous line from the movie Jerry McGuire is actually an apt description of why God made the woman. Man is made complete in his life journey with a woman by his side.

Solomon wisely said in Ecclesiastes 4:9 – *"Two are better than one, because they have a good return for their labor: If either of them falls down, one can help the other up. But pity anyone who falls and has no one to help them up. Also, if two lie down together, they will keep warm. But how can one keep warm alone?"*

Fourth, in God's design for marriage, He commanded that a man shall leave his father and his mother and hold fast to his wife, and they shall become one flesh. They were to live together in perfect unity and become one flesh.

Our invisible God made man from the dust of the earth – male and female He made them... to be united together as one flesh.

As with all of God's sacred ordinances and commands, marriage was established for man's benefit and joy, and no power in heaven or earth is exempt from God's divine institutions.

It is sad to see this sacred ordinance being violated and ignored by the world today.

The world chooses to ignore God's commands and design for love and relationships.

"Love wins" or *"we should be free to love anyone"* – they say. But God is *not* mocked. The consequences for disobedience and ignoring God's will shall come to pass whether in this world or when you face God as He sits on His throne of judgement.

God used the beautiful picture of marriage between a man and a woman as a lovely illustration of the sacred union between Christ and His bride, which is the Church.

It was Christ Who loved the church so much, that He *"gave Himself up for her, so that He might sanctify her, having cleansed her by the washing of water with the Word - and so that He might present the church to Himself in splendor, without spot or wrinkle that she might be holy and without blemish."* Ephesians 5:25-27 NKJV

So after understanding God's design for marriage, how then can a couple ensure that they are truly a match made in heaven?

As mentioned earlier, The coming together of a couple has to be according to the will and purpose of God for both individuals. It *cannot* be forced and *cannot* be only up to the couple to decide.

In our church in Manila, we often have other believers on stage share their testimonies before our pastors preach their Sunday messages. Time and time again we hear of Christians who thought they were marrying the man or woman of their dreams and then walk away from obedience to God's Word, the counsel of godly people, or to respect desires of parents.

You see if someone is truly God's gift to you, there will be no problem getting the blessing and approval from your parents and confirmation from your church Pastor.

When you start encountering people who do not believe that this is God's will, then slow down.

It is often said that "love is blind". This is why it is best to ask God for the spiritual eyes to see His will and purpose for you.

You may not like the answer you get from God and this could be emotionally painful. However, you have to trust that God has your best interest at heart. His *very* best for you is yet to come.

I would like to share the story of my son, Silas who got married to his long-time girlfriend, Nikki in 2019.

The reason I am choosing to share their story is to illustrate what I believe a match made in heaven looks like.

It is story of love that was divinely designed and orchestrated by God. A relationship that endured testing, and that took years in the making because God was still working to change their hearts and mold them to become His best gift to each other.

On their journey to marriage, I have observed a number of *principles* that could help couples today.

It will help couples who are intending to get married and those who are already married.

PRINCIPLE ONE: *Focus on your vertical relationship with God before the horizontal relationships with others.*

This was very true in the life of Silas and Nikki. They met while in University together. They became a couple then, but it was solely based on physical attraction.

They were young and full of dreams and aspirations. Both pursued their interests in studies, sports, and other leisure activities. It was all about what each of them wanted.

There existed a high degree of self-centeredness in the way they lived their individual lives.

Though they have both came to know Jesus Christ during this time, this was more head knowledge. There was no *true surrender* to Jesus as their Lord.

One piece of evidence of this was their attraction to worldly living and pursuits.

Understandably, this all led to a decision for them to part ways. It was a difficult and painful decision for both, but little did they know that the Lord was going to use this time to change their hearts.

Both Nikki and Silas went on to graduate from University and were living separate lives.

Nikki went back to her home province to seek employment and spend time with her family. Silas in the meantime stayed in Manila and started working as a stock trader.

It was during this time that the Lord was also using different people to touch their lives to become active in a church community.

Our family attends Christ Commission Fellowship (CCF) services in Manila, with satellite churches across the Philippines and the world.

Well, Silas started to actively attend a Discipleship Group which met regularly to fellowship, study God's Word, and pray for one another.

Nikki on the other hand was also involved in a small group and actually started working for the satellite church of CCF, in her home province of Cebu.

God was gloriously at work, but both did not realize what was going on.

As each of them continued to actively focus on their vertical relationship with God, He was also transforming their hearts to become attracted to the things of God rather than the things of the world.

Both were maturing in the faith which started to reflect in the way they made decisions in their personal life. There was progress in the right direction!

Faith in God became important. Focusing on obeying Scriptures became paramount. Going to worship on Sundays became a priority.

Interestingly, even though they were apart, both were actually still thinking about each other.

In time, God rekindled that initial attraction they had, and this transformed to love. Their hearts now in tune with God's will and purpose, He orchestrated events to allow them to be reunited when they both attended an international discipleship conference at CCF.

It was much later that I learned, that both my wife and Nikki's mother were praying for both to be reunited!

A match made in heaven starts with our hearts right with God.

1 Timothy 2:4 tells us that *"God desires all people to be saved and come to the knowledge of the truth."*

Each of us cannot possibly live out His will, if we have not embraced Jesus Christ as our Lord and Savior. This relationship with the Lord is critical to live according to the Lord's will and plan for our lives.

It has been said that the Christian life is *not* hard, but actually *impossible* to live without the Holy Spirit empowering and leading us.

In Ephesians 1:13 we are told that those who listen and believe in the gospel are saved and receive the Holy Spirit.

Nikki and Silas fondly call this new version of their relationship as "Nikki & Silas 2.0"!!

What changed?

Instead of the self-centeredness that characterized their prior relationship, they were now focused on God **first**…then each other.

And God did not stop in transforming their hearts and minds until the point when they could become God's best gift to each other. God wanted them to give their best selves to each other.

So what happens if you are already married? Could your union with your spouse still be a match made in heaven?

I believe that God's desire is to see man saved *first* before anything else.

The vertical relationship with God is crucial to transforming our horizontal relationships, most specially with your spouse.

As you are transformed from within – your values, motives, and thoughts start to become aligned with God's will and purposes. Your behaviors change. Your words become more loving. Your actions become more caring.

I have seen and heard of so many couples who had to endure toxic relationships before coming to the Lord. Miraculously, these same relationships supernaturally changed when God became the Third Person in the relationship.

PRINCIPLE TWO: *Honor your Father and Mother.*

With all the advances in technology and people declaring that they are free to do as they choose, this command of God is largely ignored if not downright rejected.

"Times have changed," they say. *"It's our turn,"* they say.

Young people can't wait to come of age to start making their own decisions and live their lives without the supervision of parents.

Some don't even wait to turn 18 years old and simply rebel against their parents.

Yet God does *not* change. His will and purpose for mankind does *not* change. His commands given during the time of Moses still stands during our time. It is therefore wise to take heed.

John Calvin teaches that *"God places mothers and fathers in a lofty position by* "*sharing with them part of his honor."*

Honoring our mother and father — whether or not they are Christians — is really honoring the God who gave them authority in the first place.

Bearing patiently with their failures is easier if we remember that we are ultimately honoring God **through** honoring our parents."

It took me a long time to understand this especially through the challenges I had with my father — off and on since I was a teenager. I now recognize that God calls me to honor him just because God has given him to me as my father.

We had many disagreements and didn't truly understand each other's viewpoints. That is however beside the point, because I am called to obey, honor, and respect my parents.

How can you honor your father and mother in Christian dating and relationships?

Do Christians need their parents' permission to date or marry someone?

What does the Bible say about parental approval, obeying your parents, and honoring your parents as an adult?

Many would think that this might be too old fashioned and is no longer relevant for the times. People will claim that who they see and marry is no else's business but theirs. No one should get in the way and interfere with their happiness.

But what does the Bible say?

The Bible is very clear:

"Children, obey your parents in everything, for this pleases the Lord." Colossians 3:20

"Children, obey your parents in the Lord, for this is right." Ephesians 6:1

Both verses refer to "children" who are called to obey their parents. My best understanding of the biblical use of the word "child" when referring to human families – are those people still dependent upon their parents.

If someone is still living with their parents and has not taken on adult responsibilities for themselves, I believe this is what the Bible is talking about when it says, *"Children obey your parents."*

On the other hand, *obedience* is for "everything" – including dating and relationships.

So, what happens when you are no longer living with your parents?

All Christians are still called to honor their father and mother because Exodus 20:12 states, *"Honor your father and your mother, that your days may be long in the land that the Lord your God is giving you."*

As an adult, it is *not* about seeking permission but rather their *approval* and *blessing*.

It is this act that conveys respect for your parents' opinion and wisdom. So even if you disagree with what your parents want, you must disagree in a way that is *not* disrespectful. You must seek to honor them even when you do not follow their counsel.

In the case of Nikki and Silas, they chose to willfully honor their parents on both sides by seeking their permission to date and later for their blessing to get married.

I am based in Singapore, so I was pleasantly surprised to get a video call from Silas one day indicating that he had something important to tell us.

Frankly, I was a bit concerned about wat he wanted to talk to us about. Did he get into an accident? Did he get someone pregnant?

I was very relieved and I thank God that it wasn't any of these!

My wife and I were so pleased when he asked for our approval to date Nikki again. Of course we said yes!

It was simply *so* refreshing and encouraging to see a young man who was already independent in his ways, and yet who wanted to honor us, and therefore honor God.

I distinctly remember my wife and I saying to each other that "This young man will be blessed for honoring us."

What Silas did was a *far cry* from how I approached dating and relationships when I was his age.

I simply introduced the girls I was dating to my parents, without seeking their consent or feedback. And then, when I was planning to settle down, I remember merely informing my parents that I was getting married, giving them details on when, where, etc.

I did not know the Lord Jesus then.

After seeking our permission, Silas did the same with Nikki's parents. He traveled to Nikki's home province of Cebu to seek an audience with her parents. I remember how he vulnerably related to my wife and to me how nervous he was.

Nikki's father was more concerned about Silas's intentions for Nikki which was only right. Silas assured him that his intention was to aim to become financially stable first, and then to marry Nikki. This pleased Nikki's parents and they gave their permission to Silas.

It was a couple of years later when Silas planned on proposing marriage to Nikki. He informed my wife and me, and we wholeheartedly gave him our blessing.

Unbeknownst to Nikki, he bought an engagement ring and then sought the blessing of her parents after showing them the ring he had bought for her. They were likewise very pleased to give him their approval *and* blessing.

Perhaps many of you might not be able to name someone, or you may have difficulty naming a friend, who has followed this route of honoring parents.

Silas then meticulously planned the engagement dinner.

He found a very romantic venue outside of Manila that was purposely made for "popping the question". I wasn't even aware these types of restaurants existed!

They would set up the restaurant for a specific theme, offer a custom dinner menu for two, a small signboard for any message, and would screen a movie of your choice.

Silas had everything captured on video from the moment they walked into the restaurant with Nikki visibly surprised with what was going on.

As they approached the table for two, she saw the signboard that said, "WILL YOU MARRY ME?" Immediately Silas got on his knee and we watched Nikki's excitement as she began to jump in place before and after Silas put the ring on her finger.

The next thing we saw was Silas's post on Facebook saying, "She said YES!" and a picture of the couple, with Nikki proudly showing her engagement ring.

Well, my wife and I simply teared up seeing them *so* happy. It was a long wait and here they were one step closer to getting married.

PRINCIPLE THREE: *Be intentional about honoring God.*

In 1 Corinthians 6:20 we are reminded, *"For you have been bought with a price; therefore glorify God in your body."*

We always have to bear in mind that we were *all* alienated from God, considered His enemies, and destined for His wrath *until* we were reconciled to Him through the blood that was shed on the cross for us by our Lord Jesus Christ.

A hefty price was paid for the forgiveness of our sins. It is only fitting that we glorify the Lord by being intentional about honoring Him in *everything* we do.

Romans 12:1-2 entreats us, *"Therefore I urge you, brethren, by the mercies of God, to present your bodies a living and holy sacrifice, acceptable to God, which is your spiritual service of worship. And do not be conformed to this world, but be transformed by the renewing of your mind, so that you may prove what the will of God is, that which is good and acceptable and perfect."*

Here, the apostle Paul is appealing to our wills, reminding us that God calls us to make a choice about the way that we live for Him.

We do this because of the mercy and grace God has bestowed upon us. We have been *justified* from guilt and the penalty of sin. We have been *adopted* as sons and daughters of the Lord. We are *indwelled* by the Holy Spirit. We have the *hope* of spending eternity in the Lord's presence. We have the *confidence* that nothing can separate us from the love of God.

In light of all this mercy – past, present, and future, Paul beseeches Christians to live holy lives as a fitting response to what God has done for them. We are to be living sacrifices, holy and unblemished by sin…similar to the animal sacrifices brought to the temple to the Lord in the Old Testament.

This is how we worship and honor God. "Presenting our bodies" refers to giving yourself to God. This pertains to everything about you – thoughts, words, actions. This is an ongoing sacrifice to the Lord. A life devoted to honoring God in *every* facet of our lives.

So how can one achieve this? By resisting *conformity* to the world and embracing the *transformation* that comes in Jesus Christ.

We are warned that the "world system" – the popular culture and manner of thinking that is in rebellion against God – will try to conform us to its ungodly pattern, and that process *must* be resisted.

We are commanded to be *transformed* by the renewing of our minds – which is the opposite of being *conformed* to this world.

The battle ground between conforming to the world and being transformed is *within* the mind of the believer. Christians *must* think differently.

Adherence to these commands were topmost in the minds of Nikki and Silas when they got engaged and settled on a date for their wedding a year after.

They were *very* intentional in wanting to honor God as they prepared for their wedding.

The first thing they did was inform the church of their intentions and this set in motion pre-marriage counseling sessions that they had to complete.

One of the requirements from the church was a "Covenant of Purity" that they entered into, in the sight of God and the leaders of the church.

This Covenant called for both of them to keep themselves pure for each other until their wedding day. This meant not having sexual relations and avoiding putting themselves at risk especially when they were alone.

Many again might raise their eyebrow or frown at this, believing that times have changed.

The one thing we have to bear in mind is that God does *not* change. He is the same yesterday, today, and tomorrow. As such, His commands for purity do not change.

The entire world could view pre-marital sex as acceptable, <u>but</u> it will still be *against* God's design for couples.

As Nikki and Silas intentionally chose to honor God, they also planned to have a Christian wedding where the gospel message would be central to the ceremony.

They wanted their wedding to be a testimony of their love, and the faithfulness of God.

I was genuinely honored when the couple asked me to deliver the message, and a Pastor who was close to Nikki's family was asked to solemnize the wedding.

Both sides of the family were mobilized to plan the wedding of the year.

Nikki was envisioning her dream wedding and every member of the family was eager to contribute and make this a reality.

The wedding took place in Baguio City in the northern area of the Philippines. It was a location unlike most of the Philippines because of its cool weather, mountains, and pine trees.

The wedding day came, and the couple couldn't be happier. They were surrounded by family members from *both* sides who were eager to show their love and support. This occasion was even more special because this would be the *first* wedding for both sides!

The stage was set. The outdoor setting perfect. As all were seated in eager anticipation, the music started and the entourage began walking in.

Silas was all smiles waiting for his lovely bride. He was visibly excited. The time he had been waiting for was finally here.

Then came the bride's turn to walk down the aisle. There was a curtain situated in the middle of the aisle so Silas could not see his bride.

Then the curtains were unveiled, and he looked with so much love at his wife to be. He could not help but shed tears of joy at the sight of Nikki.

The ceremony was unforgettable.

Each part of the wedding was so meaningful. There was even a little rain that added to the drama. Tears of joy from the heavens for a couple so intentional about honoring God.

I delivered the gospel message weaving in the story of their lives, much of which I covered here.

Everyone was *moved* with emotion as Nikki and Silas read their vows and then followed this up by honoring their parents.

This was not the usual custom for weddings in the Philippines. There was not one dry eye among those who were in attendance.

Then Nikki and Silas finally heard the phrase from the Pastor, "I now pronounce you man and wife." The love story *ten* years in the making was now sealed with a sweet kiss. It was a moment of unimaginable joy for the couple!

Their unwavering faith in God and love for each other was in full display.

God was intentionally honored in this celebration of love. Nikki had her dream wedding and Silas the woman of his dreams.

Surely, this was a match made in heaven.

As we surrender our hearts to God and intentionally choose to honor Him in everything we do, He transforms us to become the best version of ourselves. This is when we can relate to the ones we love, in a manner that is aligned with God's design for relationships.

So, if you want to have a match made in heaven, let God in!

Left to Right: Timothy (Patrick's son),
Leni (Patrick's beautiful wife), Nikki and Silas, Patrick

PATRICK DEL PRADO

Patrick F. del Prado currently oversees the development of leaders globally at Takeda Pharmaceuticals Inc.

He has been in the pharmaceutical industry for over 30 years serving in different country, regional and global roles.

He has also been serving the Lord as an Elder of Agape Community Christian Fellowship in the Philippines for 15 years.

Patrick also served as the previous Chairman of the Board of Christian Missions in the Philippines, Inc.

He is also a faithful member and servant in Christ Commission Fellowship. The roles he cherishes most are that of a being faithful husband to his beautiful wife, Leni, a loving father to two sons, a newbie Father-in-law, and a doting grandfather to his three adorable grandchildren.

CHAPTER 5

DIVINELY DESIGNED EKKLESIA DIVINELY DESIGNED DECLARATIONS

By Jackie Lansangan-Morey

THE EKKLESIA

"And I also say to you that you are Peter, and on this rock I will build My **ekklesia**, *and the gates of Hades shall not prevail against it."* Matthew 16:18 NASB

(Notes: "*Ekklesia*" is the original Greek word used. The above verse was spoken by Jesus to His disciples at Caesaria Philippi.)

What a bold-faced and audacious promise declared by the Lord Jesus…that the gates of Hades shall **not** prevail against the Ekklesia!!

Who is this Ekklesia and what does it mean?

Well, before I share more about this, I'd like you to know that this Chapter is *"hot off the press"* so to speak because this has been my Husband's and my recent journey to becoming Ekklesia.

Our journey began in the first quarter of 2020, it's been an adventure, here's what we've discovered, and later on in the chapter, I'll share what we've implemented in our daily lives for quite some time.

Let's begin!

Did you know that the scholars whom King James appointed to translate the Greek Bible into English in 1611 – were given specific Instructions or Rules, which they had to follow?

More on this in a few moments. Allow me to ask you another question.

Ok, what are the first *three* things you think of, when somebody mentions the word "*church*"?

Do you think of a church building – like when you say, "I left my Bible at *church*"?

Attending a church service – when someone says, "I'm going to *church*"?

Does "church" also mean a group of Christians to you, when people say, "We believers are the *church*"?

Well, if you said yes to the above three, you're *right!*

The word "*church*" is dictionary-defined as: a) a building for public worship, especially Christian worship; b) an official Christian religious organization [e.g. the Baptist church]; c) a public worship gathering; and d) the entire community of Christians.

Now, would you be *astonished* to know that when King James had the Bible translated from Greek to English, he specified *fifteen* (15) *instructions* by which the translators needed to abide?

More specifically, I'd like to draw your attention to Instruction #3:

> *#3: The old ecclesiastical words to be kept, as the word* **church**, **not** *to be translated* **congregation**.

References:

http://thekingsbible.com/Library/InstructionsToTranslators
https://www.petergoeman.com/15-rules-of-translation-for-the-king-james-version-kjv/

Instruction #3 is the one that pertains to our topic right now because King James specifically instructed that these scholars translate the Greek word "Ekklesia" into the English word *"church"* instead of the word *"congregation"*, or more importantly, the *deeper* meaning of "Ekklesia" when it was being used during the time of Jesus, which we'll talk about later.

Hmmm…why do *you* think King James specifically gave this instruction?

Want to take a guess?

Why do I bring this up?

And *why* is this important?

Off by a Few Degrees

Well, before I answer these questions, I'd like you to imagine a starting point for a race that runs on a straight track.

If Runner A takes off in a straight line, and Runner B takes off at a mere 5-degree angle off from the straight line, where would Runner B end up after 10 miles into the race?

He would be approximately ONE mile off from the track, where Runner A would be on the straight track.

How far would they be from each other, if the finish line were 20 miles from the starting line?

Well, Runner B would be almost FOUR miles off from the location of the finish line!!

And that's if Runner B took off a mere *FIVE-degrees* at an angle from the Starting line!!

Now, let's apply this to believers…Christ-followers all over the world, since 1611 – when the King James Bible was published.

If the Lord specifically meant *one* thing when He used the word "*Ekklesia*", and the word was mistranslated, or a *few degrees off* of its original meaning and intent, what happens to the general direction of the community of believers – *after many centuries*?

Yes, you guessed it!

After a period of time and the continual passing on to the following generations of the "*off-by-a-few-degrees*" meaning of a word, there are very real and dare I say, even *negative* consequences.

I'd like you to consider that possibility that this *one* Instruction *alone* (Instruction #3) has *disempowered*, *crippled*, and *emasculated* the Ekklesia for over 400 years!!

In other words, here's my *monumentally* startling claim, which I'll promptly back with some solid references:

The King James 1611 Bible, in which the Greek word "ekklesia" was translated into the English word "*church*", was an insidious mistranslation, which has *deprived* Christ-followers of the Lord's *power* and *authority* – for centuries!!

At least *since* the 1600s.

> "*The King James 1611 Bible, in which the Greek word "ekklesia" was translated into the English word "church", is an insidious mistranslation, which has deprived Christ-followers of the Lord's* **power** *and* **authority** *– for centuries!!*" ~Jackie Morey

In Dean Briggs's book "Ekklesia Rising" he writes:

"Now you see why the cultural subtext of Caesarea Philippi is critical. With all these kingdom-displacing references to rocks, might they be standing in sight of the Rock of the Gods when Jesus prompts this conversation? Is it an accident that HE speaks of assailing the gates of Hades at an earthly locale that fits the bill, a place of legend that claimed men's souls, fed their fears, inspired their worship? Did HE travel 30 miles out of HIS way for nothing?

"No, clearly Jesus is making an object lesson. The Lord of Heaven and Earth stands before twelve mortal disciples, and in a burst of insight more brilliant than the snow-capped glow of Mount Hermon, Peter becomes the first human to recognize Christ for who HE really is.

*"The Ancient of Days has come. Lord of hosts. Captain of the armies of God. The promised Messiah. **The Christ**!*

"Jesus answers Peter's revelation with, of all things, a building plan. In the Greek, He said, 'I will build my ekklesia.' Now you probably thought He pledged to build His church, right? That's what we've all been taught because that's how nearly every Bible version renders it.

*"But church is the wrong concept because it's literally the wrong word. **It's not a poor translation, but a mistranslation of the original language.** While such a suggestion is no doubt controversial, please bear with me and I'll prove it in time. Furthermore, if true, it is critical that we admit our error. Why? Because we want to discern Jesus's actual mission, not some historically entrenched mistranslation, however dear it has become to our hearts. What if the church can't actually do what Jesus said we were supposed to do? What if it takes an ekklesia?*

"'But they're the same!' you say. 'My pastor said so.'

"What if they aren't the same? Are you willing to discover the difference?

"…He cherishes His Bride, and identifies with His brothers, but what He convened in Matthew 16 and promised to build was an ekklesia, not a church.

"Since language produces culture, we will always exist at a deficit in our mission until we confront the chasm between these two words. Church produces one thing. Ekklesia produces another.

"There is no way around it: the Greek word ekklesia means something more and different than the English word 'church'. The gap is meaningful and real."

(The excerpts above are from "Ekklesia Rising" by Dean Briggs. He is a teacher, strategist and intercessor who has ministered across the nation and many nations of the earth. Formerly a pastor and church planter, he has served The Call both in national mobilization and as a trainer for the Spiritual Air Force Academy [SAFA].)

Now I get the privilege of sharing with you *why* knowing what Jesus meant when He specifically used the word "Ekklesia" is vitally important.

You see, when Jesus took His disciples to Caesaria Philippi, this place was a central location for pagan worship, child sacrifice, sex with prostitutes as their worship to their deities, and several other kinds of *powerful demonic activity* that took place there.

How *reassuring* that the Lord told His disciples that the very gates of Hades would *not prevail* against the Ekklesia that HE was building, and continues to build to this day!

Also, during that time, the definition of the word "Ekklesia" was widely known throughout the Roman empire.

Even the Jews knew what this word meant, and *everyone* during that time knew exactly what an Ekklesia meant, and what it was.

What does "Ekklesia" mean?

When you dig deeper and do your own research, you'll discover that the word "Ekklesia" doesn't only mean "called-out ones".

Its full meaning encompasses all the rights, responsibilities, power and authority of a *"Governing council,"* a *"Ruling council"* and a *"Legislative council"*.

When the Lord Jesus said He would build His Ekklesia, He meant that He would **build** His own *"Governing, Ruling, Legislative, Divine Council"* and then **empower** *this* Ekklesia with HIS full authority and demonstration of His power!

I'm writing all this because I want to inspire *you* to hunger for more, to get trained in becoming Ekklesia, so that you can move in HIS power and authority, such that you and I will see and experience signs, wonders, miracles and *more* of the supernatural than ever before…and we'll faithfully give *all* the glory and honor to HIM!!

In renowned evangelist Ed Silvoso's book "Ekklesia" he states:

> *"The ekklesia was…first developed as a ruling assembly of citizens in the Grecian democracy to govern its city-states.*

> *"When the more hierarchical Romans replaced the Greeks in the imperial scene, the Romans assimilated the concept. Consequently, the general public in Jesus' day understood ekklesia to mean both the secular institution and the governmental system it represented.*

> *"The Greek and Roman versions of the ekklesia appeared in different forms and sizes, all of which are relevant to the subject at hand. But one form is especially notable: the* **Conventus Civium Romanorum**, *or* **conventus** *for short. According to Sir William Ramsay, when a group of Roman citizens as small* **as two or three gathered anywhere in the world**, *it constituted the* **conventus** *as a local expression of Rome.*

> *"Even though geography separated them from the capital of the empire and the emperor, their coming together as fellow citizens automatically brought the power and presence of Rome into their midst. This was indeed the Roman ekklesia in a microcosm.*

> *"In the same manner that Rome made its presence, power and culture felt in*

*the far reaches of its empire, **Jesus designed His Ekklesia to make its presence, power and culture known**, but with a revolutionary caveat that gave it the upper hand: It would have the authority to legislate in **both the visible and invisible realms** so that the Gates of Hades could not prevail in either realm."*

(The excerpts above are from "Ekklesia" by Dr. Ed Silvoso. He is a bestselling author trained in both theology and business, is the founder and president of Harvest Evangelism and leader of the Transform Our World Network.)

I hope I've piqued your curiosity to the point that you're hungering to learn more, and become Ekklesia.

For example: What if I told you that in China, the persecuted underground Ekklesia there has been experiencing miracles that the body of Christ in the West has not experienced on a regular basis, or has *rarely* seen?

How often have we heard of people instantly healed, or even being raised from the dead?

It is *rare* indeed, right?

Well, *not* in the underground, persecuted body of Christ-followers in China.

Now consider another of Jesus's audacious statements in John 14:12-14:

*"I tell you the truth, anyone who believes in Me will do the **same works I have done, and even greater works**, because I am going to be with the Father. You can **ask for anything** in my Name, and I will do it, so that the Son can bring glory to the Father. Yes, ask Me for anything in My Name, and I will do it!"*

Have we in the Western church dared to believe for, or do we experience on a regular basis, these kinds of miracles – the raising of the dead, blind eyes opened, the lame instantly healed?

If not, why not?

I'm not saying this to point a finger of criticism at the body of Christ in the West...*not at all.*

My motivation for sharing these things is to provoke us – you *and* me – to godly jealousy, and to inspire us to hunger and desire for more – oh, **so** much more!!

Allow me to ask: Have you and I experienced doing "***greater works***" than the Lord Jesus's works, that HE said HE would do through us, greater works which HE died and paid for?

Have we instantly been used to ***heal*** people with heart disease, diabetes, back pain, kidney disease, those dying of cancer, etc.?

Have we been used by GOD to heal those who are mute, blind from birth, crippled from birth, or those terminally ill?

Have we seen limbs grow when we've prayed for those whose arms, legs or other body parts had been amputated?

Have we prayed for people and they are instantly ***healed*** from experiencing *years of trauma*, just like Mary Magdalene was instantly healed?

Or is our ***only*** expectation that it will take people who have undergone trauma, tremendous abuse, rejection, betrayal, or those who have been addicted to drugs, alcohol, pornography, gambling, etc. – *years and years* of counseling and therapy?

Now please hear my heart. I'm *not* devaluing the excellent and wonderful Christian counselors, mental health therapists and social workers...not at all.

In fact, I personally know some of them, they're my good friends, and I profoundly appreciate *them* and *all* the work they've done for several years to help many people receive emotional and inner healing from horrendous traumas!

Here's my point.

I'm genuinely inviting you to *consider* the possibility of thinking "*outside the box*" so to speak, and to think from Heaven's perspective, because we're on the other side of the Cross, and we have a *far* better covenant.

In other words, let's ask ourselves: What *all* did the Lord Jesus die and pay for when He rose from the dead and in both Matthew and Mark gave us believers, a comprehensive Commission, which includes the *discipling of entire nations*?

What "greater works" may we ask for, expect, and believe for – *this* side of glory?

Might we dare believe for miracles? Or do we think these were only meant for those who are "clergy members," those who have titles?

I'd like to posit that when the Lord Jesus gave the "Great Commission" in both Matthew and Mark, He meant it for *all* believers – that means you and me, and not merely those who are "clergy" or pastors, or salaried staff members at church communities.

May I boldly say with *deep respect*, that we *don't* need to be in the 5-fold ministry, we don't need to be in any church hierarchy, and we don't need to enroll in seminary, to be *vessels* for these kinds of *gloriously miraculous signs and wonders*!!

The Great Commission is for *every* Christian.

Isn't this encouraging and inspiring to know?

The Lord Jesus's commission in Matthew 28 and Mark 16 were meant for *all* believers, all Christ-followers, all true disciples.

Ok, this next question may cause your jaw to drop…

Did you know that there are trustworthy testimonies of children walking on water in China because when the monsoon rains flooded some of their towns, the bridges were washed out, and these children wanted to cross to the other towns *far away* – to tell those people about the Lord Jesus and preach the Gospel?

These are children who are not pastors nor Bible teachers. They are fairly new believers, and yet they've walked on water, and have experienced miraculous signs and wonders that neither I nor most of us believers in the West have seen nor experienced.

According to the testimony, these children were utterly committed to preaching the Gospel to the faraway towns that they walked toward these towns.

And when they encountered the monsoon floods, they asked the Lord to help them cross over the flood waters to get to these other towns, so that they could tell multitudes of people about the Lord Jesus Christ. Miracle of miracles, they walked on water indeed and got to share the Good News about the LORD!!

You see, I'm hungry and thirsty to advance the Lord's kingdom by being a vessel of His miraculous signs and wonders.

Because *after* we meet people's most pressing needs in a miraculous and supernatural way, it is far easier for them to believe, acknowledge and receive the Lord Jesus as their personal Lord and Savior.

What about you…are you hungry and thirsty for more as well?

At present, merely leaving Christian tracts or handing someone a Gospel tract will *not* be effective as they were in the past.

Why not?

People are hungry for the supernatural, they want to know that there is a GOD Who specifically cares about them, where they are at, and about their most pressing needs.

Do you think handing a gospel tract to an atheist, a Muslim or a Buddhist would be effective?

They're more likely to throw it out or leave it somewhere for someone else, but not for themselves.

Why?

Because *for them*, it has no direct relevance to their lives.

If we look at the Lord Jesus's example, what did HE do such that people followed Him and many believed in Him as their Savior?

He went about doing good – casting out demons, healing the sick, opening blind eyes, unstopping deaf ears, healing lepers, raising the dead, sharing a word of knowledge to the woman at the well in the Gospel of John Chapter 4 and even *miraculously feeding thousands* of people by multiplying a few loaves and fishes!!

In other words, He first met people's needs everywhere He went, He shared words of knowledge, He set people free from demonic possession and oppression, He prophesied, and He performed signs, wonders and miracles!!

I wholeheartedly believe that as the Ekklesia of the Lord, as representatives of His kingdom, those who are called to occupy and extend His kingdom to all areas of society, we are commissioned to do the same.

And we, the Ekklesia, can expect these signs, wonders and miracles to be much more commonplace as more and more Christ-followers take their place in the Governing, Divine Ruling Council of GOD.

As the Ekklesia of the Lord Jesus, Who is also Lord Sabbaoth or the Lord of Heaven's Armies, we have the honor and the mandate to legislate, to govern, to decree, to forbid things that are not in line with what is already in heaven…and to allow, loose and permit other things that already exist or are in line with heaven.

Do you remember when the Lord said, *"Whatever you forbid on earth will be forbidden in heaven, and whatever you loose on earth will be loosed in heaven."*

Well, here's a *more accurate translation:*

Whatever is already forbidden in heaven, forbid these on earth. And whatever is already permitted in heaven, loose and permit these on earth.

Does this help you make more sense of this verse? Wonderful!

One of the primary responsibilities of each member of an Ekklesia is to take their place in a group of at least two, three or more believers, and to *decree*, to *legislate* and to *make declarations* that are already permitted in heaven, and also to forbid on earth (your home, neighborhood, your city, state and nation) what is forbidden in heaven.

The Lord promised that when two or more of you are gathered in the Lord's Name, HE is there in your midst. And *you* are HIS divine governing, ruling council.

It is *your* right, *your* responsibility and CHRIST's mandate to you – to use your voice to make decrees so that you can *forbid* demonic activity, you can forbid the enemy's plans to trespass into your home, your relationships, your cities, your places of business and ministry, and instead, you can take more territory for our King.

1 Peter 2:9 reminds you who you are:

"…you are a chosen generation, a *royal priesthood*, a holy nation, His own special people, that you may proclaim the praises of Him who called you out of darkness into His marvelous light."

Not only are you a priest to our God, you are also *royalty!*

Do you know what kings and queens do?

One of their important rights and responsibilities is that they stretch out their scepters and make decrees!! Yes, they legislate, and proclaim declarations!

You are called to do exactly these things – as LORD Sabbaoth's royal priest and Ekklesia (His governing, divine ruling council)!!

Ok, one more scripture, and then I'll share with you examples of Divinely Designed Declarations that I've written out for you – so that you can begin to decree and legislate now, as part of HIS Ekklesia.

These Divinely Designed Declarations are some of the many that I declare and decree over my Husband, myself, our children, our extended family members and our friends, and we have experienced many answers to these decrees and declarations.

Let's look closely at what Job 22:28 states in two different versions:

"You will also **declare** a thing,
And it will be established for you;
So light will shine on your ways." Job 22:28 NKJV

"You will also **decree** a thing, and it will be established for you;
And light will shine on your ways." Job 22:28 NASB

One of the most powerful and exciting ways that the gates of Hades shall not prevail against the Lord Jesus's Ekklesia (Divine Ruling Council) is when two or three are gathered together in His Name, and they begin speaking, declaring and legislating on behalf of Heaven – forbidding on earth what is already forbidden in heaven, and permitting or loosing on earth was is already permitted in heaven!

As promised earlier, in this final section of this Chapter, I'll share what we've implemented in our daily lives.

As the Ekklesia – Lord Sabbaoth's "Divine Ruling Council," our prayers have been raised to another level. Not only are we lifting up supplications, or thanking the Lord in advance for future answers to prayer – which are important.

Whenever two or three of us gather together in HIS Name, we as the Ekklesia make decrees, we forbid on earth things that currently exist on earth, but which we know are already forbidden in heaven. We permit and loose things on earth, which we know already exist in heaven!

In other words, we decree, we declare, we pray, and we legislate.

After you've read some of the decrees I get to share below, I invite you to begin using these decrees in your own life.

I also invite you to look up more Scriptures that you could use to make your own decrees and to legislate and declare into specific situations, relationships, and the issues in your home, neighborhood, city, state and nation that concern you and your loved ones.

DIVINELY DESIGNED DECLARATIONS

As the Ekklesia of the Lord Jesus Christ, Who is Lord Sabbaoth, the Lord of Heaven's Armies, we are called and commissioned to *govern, legislate* and *decree* things, that we know have been approved in heaven and that already exist in heaven.

We're *also* called and commissioned to govern, legislate and decree things that are forbidden in heaven. We are called to *forbid, bind, handcuff* and *disallow* those things that are not approved in heaven or that don't exist in heaven.

If we fully realized the power and authority given to the Ekklesia by the Lord Jesus Christ, I believe that we would see many signs and wonders, we would experience becoming HIS vessels for multitudes of others to experience many more miracles.

We would see people instantly healed, we would be used to open blind eyes, unstop deaf ears, cast out demons, deliver those who are oppressed, bring supernatural healing to those who have experienced horrendous trauma, raise the dead, and lead hundreds if not thousands and hundreds of thousands to the Lord Jesus.

Isn't that an incredibly exciting thought? Well, let's not let it simply be a *thought.*

Let's begin here and now, to activate this in our lives.

The Decade of the 2020s is the Decade of PEY. Pey is the Hebrew word for "*mouth.*"

So many proven, trustworthy prophetic voices have shared that during this decade of the 2020s, the Lord will perform through His Christ-followers such incredible, jaw-dropping signs and wonders that we haven't even imagined!!

And because believers are the Body of Christ, we are expected by the Lord to bring heaven to earth – by using our *mouths* to **decree**, **declare** and **legislate** things that have been on the Lord Sabbaoth's plans and His heart for our cities, our states, our nation, and the nations of the world.

It is my desire that as you read this chapter, you'll be inspired and encouraged to use your mouth, your voice, the powerful Word of God (scriptures), and prophetic words to advance His kingdom, bring down strongholds, change the atmosphere, legislate HIS will, work in collaboration with His warring and ministering angels to *take back* territory, and *take more* territory for our King and His kingdom.

What does this look like?

Well, we can declare, legislate and decree into these different spheres of society:

1. The Family Sphere
2. The Government and Political Sphere
3. The Religion Sphere
4. The Arts & Entertainment Sphere
5. The Education Sphere
6. The Business Sphere
7. The Science and Technology Sphere

A great way to start is to begin using Scriptures to decree and legislate into these different Spheres of society, wherein you want to see transformation.

The Declarations below are mainly for people in your family, of for your friends. That said, if you know friends who also work in these other spheres, you may decree these declarations for them as well.

And when you pray, declare and decree, remember that there's *more power* when at least *two or three of you gather together and agree* regarding these declarations.

Declarations for Divine Healing

Lord, we declare over [person's name] the Word of God which says that the Lord Jesus was wounded for our transgressions, He was bruised for our iniquities, the chastisement of our peace was upon Him, and by His stripes, we are healed.

We decree that by the stripes that Jesus suffered, [person's name] is healed.

We also declare supernatural, diving healing over you, and we decree that No weapon formed against you shall prosper, and every tongue that rises up against you will be shown to be wrong.

Declarations for Divine Protection

(Based on the Word of God in Psalm 91)

Lord, we ask that You hide us in the secret place of the Most High God. Help us to abide under Your shadow Almighty Father. We say of You, Lord, "You are our Refuge, You are our strong Fortress of protection, You are our God, it is in You that we trust.

Surely You shall deliver us from the snare of the fowler, and from the perilous pestilence. You shall cover us with Your feathers, and under Your wings we shall take refuge; Your truth shall be your shield and buckler.

We shall not be afraid of the terror by night, nor of the arrow that flies by day, nor of the pestilence that walks in darkness, nor of the destruction that lays waste at noonday.

Thank You, Lord – that a thousand may fall at our side, and ten thousand at our right hand; But it shall not come near us. Only with our eyes shall we look, and see the reward of the wicked.

Because we have made You, Lord – our refuge, even You, the Most High, our dwelling place, I thank you that no evil shall befall us, nor shall any plague come near our dwelling; For You shall give Your angels charge over us, to keep us in all your ways. In their hands they shall bear us up, lest we dash our foot against a stone.

We shall tread upon the lion and the cobra, the young lion and the serpent you shall trample underfoot.

Because we have set our love upon You, therefore You will deliver us; You will set us on high, because we have known Your name.

We shall call upon You, and You will answer us; You will be with us in trouble; You will deliver us and honor us. With long life You will satisfy us, and show us Your salvation.

We declare this in the Name of the Lord Jesus, amen!!

Declarations for Supernatural Favor

We decree that you are covered with the Lord's supernatural favor, and that HIS favor surrounds you as a shield according to Psalm 5:12 (NIV) which says, *"Surely, Lord, you bless the righteous; You surround them with Your favor as with a shield."*

May HIS supernatural favor surround you and go with you as you meet new people, have conversations, make presentations, and collaborate with team members, clients, peers, managers, group members, neighbors, acquaintances, and friends. We decree that God's supernatural favor will eventually result in financial abundance for you.

We declare that your ways please the Lord, and because of this, the Lord will make even your enemies at peace with you according to Proverbs 16:7.

Regarding all doors which have been kept shut by the enemy in the past seasons, which God has ordained to be opened now, we decree that all these doors be opened for you now, in the authority of the Lord Jesus's Name!!

We declare new business, personal and ministry relationships which the Lord has ordained for you to be connected with. We decree that you will find supernatural favor with those whom you already know, that are meant to connect you to these new relationships, and that these connectors will remember you.

We declare that they will not be able to resist the favor of God that is upon you, and that they will promptly introduce you to these new relationships, so that you can collaborate with them and accomplish all that the LORD has ordained for you to achieve with them.

We ask, declare and decree all these things in the authority and the Name of the Lord Jesus Christ, amen!

Declarations for Wisdom, Intelligence and Direction

Lord, we ask You according to James 1:5, to please download Your wisdom to [name of the person you're praying for who needs wisdom and guidance].

You said in Your Word that whoever needs wisdom, let that person ask of YOU, Lord, and you would lavishly and generously give Your wisdom, without reproach, without finding fault. I believe and receive Your wisdom now for [name the person you're praying for who needs wisdom and guidance].

We pray and declare Ephesian 1:17, that the God of our Lord Jesus Christ, the Father of glory, may give to you [name the person] the spirit of wisdom and revelation in the knowledge of Him.

We declare Isaiah 11:2 over you. That the Spirit of the Lord will rest on you — the Spirit of wisdom and of understanding, the Spirit of counsel and of might, the Spirit of the knowledge and fear of the Lord—and that you will delight in the fear of the Lord.

Thank You, Lord – in Jesus's Name, amen.

Declarations for Financial Provision

We decree that you receive unexpected divine provision and financial resources now in the authority of the Lord Jesus Christ.

We declare Deuteronomy 1:11 NIV over you which says: *"May the Lord, the God of your ancestors, increase you a thousand times and bless you as He has promised!"*

May the Lord multiply and increase you a thousand-fold in your finances, in your relationships, in your contacts, projects, contracts and provision.

Lord, we ask You according to James 1:5, to please download Your wisdom to [name of the person you're praying for who needs wisdom and guidance]. You said in Your Word that whoever needs wisdom, let that person ask of YOU, Lord, and you would lavishly and generously give Your wisdom, without reproach, without finding fault. We believe and receive Your wisdom now for [name of the person you're praying for who needs wisdom and guidance].

We declare that you receive witty ideas, inventions and revenue-generating ideas from the Lord. We decree that projects, employment opportunities, and doors of financial provision open up for you *now* that are from the Lord. We shut doors that are not from the Lord.

We decree that you are covered with the Lord's supernatural favor, and that HIS favor surrounds you as a shield according to Psalm 5:12 (NIV) which says, *"Surely, Lord, you bless the righteous; You surround them with Your favor as with a shield."*

May HIS supernatural favor surround you and go with you as you write emails, connect with people, go to interviews, have conversations and attend meetings that will lead to projects, contracts, the right employment, and financial abundance for you.

We ask, declare and decree all these things in the authority and the Name of the Lord Jesus Christ, amen!

Declarations for Restoration

Father GOD, in the Name of the Lord Jesus, we declare and decree Joel 2:25 over [name of person you're interceding for], that he/she experiences YOUR restoration from the years that the swarming locust, the crawling locust, the consuming locust, and the chewing locust have eaten.

We forbid and break the power of destruction and attack in the Name of the Lord Jesus.

We decree Isaiah 61:4, the rebuilding of ruins, and the repairing of cities in the life of [name of person you're interceding for].

We pray that [name of person you're interceding for] receives restitution, reimbursements, payback and benefits. We declare great success, fulfillment, and rich satisfaction.

We decree that all that the Lord has planned in this new season for [person's name] life, will manifest now in the Name of the Lord Jesus Christ. Amen!

Declarations for Prodigals to Return

We declare and decree that your prodigal [son / daughter / niece / nephew / cousin / brother / sister / family member(s) – call out their name(s)] return(s) to the Lord.

We pray and decree that they receive revelation from the Spirit of wisdom and revelation, insight, knowledge and counsel so that they would renew a right relationship with GOD.

We break the power of every demonic spirit from operating in [name the person]'s life in the mighty Name of the Lord Jesus Christ, by the authority He gave to me.

We forbid all spirits of lying, deception, manipulation and control from operating any longer in your [son's / daughter's / niece's / nephew's / cousin's / brother's / sister's / family member's life] from this moment forward, according to the authority given to me by the LORD Jesus in Mark 16:17~18 and Matthew 16:19.

Lord, we ask by Your Spirit, to give your [son / daughter / niece / nephew / cousin / brother / sister / family member] the supernatural gift of repentance. Please open their blind eyes, unstop their deaf ears, and please plow up by your Holy Spirit, the ground of their hearts so that they can have the capacity to receive Your amazing gift of repentance.

We also ask the Lord of the Harvest, to send harvest worker-believers into the life of your [son / daughter / niece / nephew / cousin / brother / sister / family member], to send different kinds of people whom he/she will listen to.

We decree that these believers who will be placed in their path will speak words of truth, words of life, and will minister God's abundant love in a way that your [son / daughter / niece / nephew / cousin / brother / sister / family member] can and will easily receive all these, and will turn from darkness to light, from bondage to freedom, from bitterness and hatred to Abba Father's transforming love.

We declare that your [son / daughter / niece / nephew / cousin / brother / sister / family member] will return to healthy relationships with trustworthy believers in the Body of Christ, and I decree that all toxic and evil relationships are severed now in Jesus's mighty Name.

We declare that your prodigal returns home now, and the season for celebration begins, in the Name of the Lord Jesus Christ!

FINAL THOUGHTS

I hope the above declarations and decrees will inspire you to look up *more* Scriptures for yourself and your loved ones, which you could use to legislate, govern, and decree that will…

…**shift** atmospheres

…cause **breakthroughs**

…help take back and then **occupy more territory** for the King

…and **bring the kingdom of God** to every circumstance, to the people in your spheres of influence, and the places wherein you are led to intercede and legislate.

My Husband and I have been part of a Monday Ekklesia, and a Friday War Room Ekklesia, and we most certainly use these kinds of declarations and decrees to bind and loose, forbid and permit things in our relationships, cities, states and our nation.

We have experienced incredible answers to these decrees!

Well, thank you very much for allowing me to share a bit of my "Divinely Designed" journey to becoming Ekklesia.

Remember, the Lord Jesus's inheritance includes entire nations. And as HIS Ekklesia, we are called to disciple nations.

We can start here and now by decreeing, legislating, governing and ruling on behalf of LORD Sabbaoth.

MY BOOK RECOMMENDATIONS FOR YOU

1. Ekklesia Rising by Dean Briggs – https://amzn.to/2CqotvR
2. Ekklesia – Rediscovering God's Instrument for Global Transformation by Ed Silvoso – https://amzn.to/2WEsqnm
3. Daily Decrees by Brenda Kunneman – https://amzn.to/2WG1ZxO

Please email me at CustomerStrategyAcademy@gmail.com if you have any testimonies regarding these Divinely Designed Declarations. I'd love to celebrate with you.

May the Lord "multiply you a thousand times more and bless you" according to Deuteronomy 1:11.

Jackie with her husband Jim and their children Michael and Alyssa

JACKIE LANSANGAN–MOREY

Jackie is a premier entrepreneur, multiple #1 International Bestselling Author, Business Strategist, Executive Coach, Transformational Life Coach extraordinaire and Prophetic Mentor.

She's also a Book Publisher, WebTV Host and Producer of "Jackie Morey LIVE", "The 21st Century Legacy Letters", and "The Exponential You", and the Founder and CEO of Customer Strategy Academy.

Her passion is to help leaders, consultants, coaches, business professionals, medical professionals, writers and entrepreneurs – to grow their business & live their life purposefully and by design, not by default, to succeed, thrive, and flourish through her Business and Life Coaching, Book Publishing, and Online Marketing businesses.

As a degreed Engineer, she brings her unique logical expertise to simplify the nuts and bolts of self-publishing.

Her mission is to help you grow your business & live your life on purpose.

Jackie is a recognized Revenue-Generator, Relationship Ambassador, Topnotch Solution Provider, Creative Problem-solver, Peacemaker, and Team-builder.

She enjoys movies, gourmet dark chocolate, traveling, jazz, pop and classical music, chess, writing, watching movies, bike riding, volleyball, table tennis, having coffee with family and friends, eating sweet, juicy Philippine mangoes, snorkeling in the tropical beaches of Coron, Palawan, and sharing prophetic words for family members, friends, her church community, and occasionally, with complete strangers whom the Lord leads her to share a prophetic word.

She's happily married and lives in a beautiful Pacific Northwest suburb of Seattle with her husband Jim. They have a son and a daughter who "make them proud" every day.

Connect with Jackie:

Facebook: www.facebook.com/JackieMorey77
LinkedIn: www.linkedin.com/in/jackiemorey1
Twitter: www.Twitter.com/JackieMorey1

CHAPTER 6

DIVINELY DESIGNED RESTORATION

By Mildred Borbon Osias

DISINTEGRATING WALLS

Beneath an overcast sky I stood staring at the remains of the Berlin wall.

My family and I, on vacation, followed the path where the once towering formidable wall stood from 1961 to 1989, encapsulating Eastern Europe in its iron curtain.[1]

An overwhelming surge of emotion gripped me as I let my eyes gaze on the vast territory which was once imprisoned, but now takes pleasure in its liberty.

I could be standing on a spot where people lost their lives trying to cross the dividing wall that alienated them from their loved ones and families.

How could men construe such divisive ideas in their heads?

How could it be possible for evil to consume the very core of men who deliberately endeavor to wipe particular races?

---

[1] Wikipedia. Berlin Wall. 2008 August (https://en.wikipedia.org/wiki/BerlinWall)

How much horror are we capable of committing?

I have never physically murdered anyone. I have never built a visible wall. But I realized that I stood before a monument in history that embodied the hearts of many people.

I myself have allowed pain and hate to curtail living relationships and enclose me inside invisible walls – a typical story of the masses.

I shed a tear on a piece of broken wall, not just for those whose broken lives were represented by this historical piece on this terra firma, but for me and the millions who have surrounded themselves inside their own daunting walls.

While the memories of the past fused with my present, I remembered a story in the Bible that epitomized this – Jesus' encounter with the Samaritan woman in John chapter 4.

Jesus deliberately walked through a territory abominable to the Jews two thousand years ago.

He was exhausted and thirsty and sat beside Jacob's well in Samaria. He was at a place where a soaring solid wall separated the Jews and the Samaritans.

From the Jewish perspective, they had many reasons to hate the Samaritans…

When the Northern Kingdom of Israel or Samaria fell into the hands of the Assyrians, the Assyrians intermarried with many Jews of Samaria. Their offspring were considered half-breeds by the pure Jews. During the Maccabean revolt, the Samaritans supported the Assyrians against the Jews. They also rejected the custom of worshipping on Mt. Moriah in Jerusalem and declared their own holy mountain, Mt. Gerizim.[2]

---

[2] The Word in Life Study Bible, New Testament Edition, (Thomas Nelson Publishers, Nashville; 1993), pp. 340-341

The animosity was mutual. Jesus was purposefully there to disintegrate walls.

It must have been a startling surprise for the Samaritan woman to find a Jewish man sitting wearily beside the well when she deliberately came in the middle of the day expecting to not find anyone.

There were several barriers that divided them.

Jesus was a Jew. She was a Samaritan.

The enmity between these two peoples had existed for ages. To this day, men have persisted in keeping that wall. Samaria is at the West Bank, a territory being fought over by Israel and Palestine.

Moreover, Jesus was a man. She was a woman.

As time had passed, the role and status of women had deteriorated. In the New Testament there were belittling expectations of women that were non-existent in the Old Testament.

Above all else, He was a moral man. She was immoral.

Her life was disgusting, most especially to herself.

Jesus was gaining popularity for being sent from heaven, teaching God's Word with authority, healing people and performing miracles.

Every sense in her body warned of a forthcoming discord.

She expected condescension. She was used to it. That was why she came to the well at the hottest hour of the day when it was certain that no one would be around.

She was tired of the gossip whispered behind and in front of her.

Everyone knew of all her five failed relationships and her present immoral relationship with a man, who offered his bed, but not his home, the warmth of his body but not the warmth of his heart, his possessions, but not his name.

She settled for what she could get because she needed to be with someone.

No matter how dysfunctional and artificial, she gained a false sense of security and a temporary source of intimacy that her soul acutely desired for.

She must have been an immensely lovely woman for five men to want to marry her. But what was she doing wrong that she couldn't keep them?

Had she not asked that question a thousand times? Was she just a piece of meat that was worth nothing but to be devoured?

To this day, many of us long for what the Samaritan woman longed for – intimate love.

Sometimes it is so easy for us to judge sexual promiscuity not knowing why people even engage in it. Maybe it is pure lust for some. But I believe many people surrender themselves to a moment of physical intimacy to fill up the void of a real soul partnership.

The Samaritan woman was already painfully intimate with rejection. She heard the slam of the door to her face five times.

She braced herself for the encounter with this Jewish man at the well.

Respect and genuine love - these were things she did not expect.

In the short period of their discourse, this man had treated her with utmost honor. For the first time in her life, a man did not stare at her face and body but looked deep into her soul.

Jesus' interaction with women was quite avantgarde during that time. His purpose was to restore women to their original status of value and importance.

Jesus did not care that she was a Samaritan, He didn't care that she was a woman and He didn't care that she was shunned by society.

He deeply cared that she was a person thirsty for real life. Therefore, He offered her the living water of salvation.

He even took time to explain what He could offer.

Even when she was so confused as to what the living water was, Jesus patiently clarified.

One short encounter with Jesus and the walls that divided them came crashing down, until none was left.

Her soul was bare and exposed before Him but she did not feel shame or guilt. Instead she felt forgiveness, acceptance and hope.

She knew she was morally depraved, yet here was a Man who accepted her as someone who could change. He trusted in her ability to love God back. He had faith in her nature of being capable of surrendering her life to God. He did not judge her from the first moment they met but He looked at her with hope.

He had an ardent desire to chip a crack on the wall from the very first moment. This transforming encounter with the love, grace and mercy of God obliterated all barriers.

She again found that life could be found elsewhere than in the shallow love that men could provide. The love that came with caresses was insubstantial compared to the love of God that dwelt in her heart for eternity.

She went back to the people she had hidden her face from.

She acquired concern and love for the people who looked down on her and hurt her.

Her need for love that was fully satisfied by the love of God opened her eyes to other people's needs for the greatest love.

She didn't tarry or hesitate.

She immediately went back and even left her jar of water that now succumbed to the priority of reaching out to people.

She went back into town and told a multitude of Samaritans about Jesus.

With one encounter, she was stripped of her poor self-worth and instead, saw herself precious before the King of kings. There was no longer humiliation or disgrace under the veil of grace and mercy.

John 4:39-42 (NIV) states, *"Many of the Samaritans from that town believed in Him because of the woman's testimony, 'He told me everything I ever did.' They said to the woman, 'We no longer believe just because of what you said; now we have heard for ourselves, and we know that this man really is the Savior of the world.'"*

When they met Him as she did, they could not deny the supremacy of His grace and affection. His mercy drew men to Him and His love transformed their vile hearts to one that was capable of unconditional love.

He tore down the walls one by one until nothing was left to keep them apart.

On November 9, 1989 people came to the Berlin wall with various tools to collapse it. They were nicknamed 'Mauerspechte' or wall woodpeckers in English.[3]

Thousands of wall woodpeckers came chipping off the wall all together. Some had huge mallets. Some had small hammers. Some had tiny sledgehammers. But each of them passionate enough to chip off the wall.

The 96-mile long wall that divided Germany came crashing down!

We have a God who hates walls.

He sent His Son Jesus to collapse the most formidable of all – the one that divides us from Him.

In the same way, He expects us to disintegrate walls.

---

[3] History. Berlin Wall. 2010 July (https://www.history.com/topics/cold-war/berlin-wall)

On our own, it is hard to bring down these daunting walls.

But even with the smallest tool of God-empowered acts of kindness and love in our hand, we can contribute to collapsing barriers and disintegrating walls.

Through the power of God, we can bring down obstacles that keep us away from Him and from each other.

I stood before the shrine of the Berlin Wall – a small part of the wall that represented the long and towering wall that divided people for decades, and I wept.

I wept – for in my life, I saw the bricks that I myself had erected one on top of the other, slowly disintegrate before my eyes.

I too, surprisingly met this Man, waiting for me in my hostile territory.

And He looked at me, not with judgment but with tender eyes of love and mercy.

Wall woodpecker Andree Werder
from Winsen (Luhe)
in November 1989 at the Berlin Wall
on the Ebertstraße[4]

---

[4] Wall woodpecker. November 1989 at the Berlin Wall on the Ebertstraße
(https://commons.wikimedia.org/wiki/File:Mauerspecht_Andree_Werder_im_November_198
9_an_der_Berliner_Mauer.jpg)

BEAUTY IN FRAILTY

I hate plastic. I love drinking from glass.

Even when we were incredibly young, my mom would use porcelain for our dinner settings and fine glass for our drinks.

She was so unlike most Filipinos who would use melamine or plastic and reserve the fine china for visitors.

The risk however was, as children, we were prone to breaking glass. Yet despite their frailty, it did not stop my mother from truly appreciating their beauty.

A lot of beautiful things in life are so fragile.

I have been visiting Bispebjerg cemetery in Copenhagen, not only as a memorial to our youngest daughter, Adrianne, but also to look at the beautiful lane of cherry blossoms every springtime.

It takes a year to wait for the lovely blossoms that only last for fourteen days.

Hundreds of pictures cannot fully capture this fragile splendor.

OUR FRAILTY

As human beings, we are filled with brokenness.

We are shattered, by our own doings or things done to us by others, and from pursuing things we think we need the most.

Our world testifies of our brokenness through songs about broken hearts, loneliness and our never-ending pursuit to love and be loved.

Advertisements swarm us with things we "need" to own and we allow ourselves to get swayed by them. We focus on surrounding ourselves with things and achievements to fill an emptiness in our hearts.

It is not bad to want to be educated. It is not bad to find a wonderful partner in life. It is not bad to have money and live comfortably. It is not bad to have a position and power.

In fact, all of these are exceptionally good.

However, the good can be the enemy of the best, when we anchor our happiness and fulfilment on these things.

Because we live in an imperfect world, everything in it is incapable of completing us.

Only the presence of God in our lives can truly bring beauty in our frailty.

The irony is, when we follow God, He does not only restore us into something greater, but the things we relentlessly pursue, start following us instead.

Matthew 6:33 TPT

"So above all, constantly chase after the realm of God's kingdom and the righteousness that proceeds from Him. Then all these less important things will be given to you abundantly."

We get broken from what we think we lack, yet God has promised to be our Great Shepherd who will provide for what we truly need.

How does this verse translate in our real life?

Putting God first is a relational issue.

Knowing more about God or being active in church activities are not the same as having a living interactive relationship with God.

Our activities are only vessels of expressing our intimacy with God. They become the framework that makes our faith visible. Our lives become a "virtuous cycle" wherein our intimacy with God is articulated in our words, activities, lifestyle and choices.

For example, we need love, yet we forget that with God, love is not something we need to beg for. God generously gives His love freely, yet we always settle for a love that we can tangibly feel with our five senses. We lose our ability to perceive the greatest and most special love as we focus on temporal affection.

With God, we do not have to fulfil conditions in order to be loved. There is nothing we can do to make God love us more, or less because His love is perfect and everlasting.

King David knew this for certain when he said in Psalm 23:6, *"Surely goodness and lovingkindness will follow me all the days of my life, and I will dwell in the house of the LORD forever."*

God assured Israel, *"I have loved you with an everlasting love; I have drawn you with unfailing kindness."* (Jeremiah 31:3 NKJV)

> *"And even when we were rebellious against God, He demonstrated his own love for us in this: While we were still sinners, Christ died for us."* (Romans 5:8 NIV)

The astounding truth is that we keep waiting for water from a faucet, when it is already raining outside!

God does not only love us but He surrounds us with love.

Unfortunately, we wait for love from specific people and miss out on all the affection God showers us from all over. It could come from a nice clerk, a loyal friend, generous relatives, and the like.

The enemy likes to downplay everything regarding God. He steals the fantastic and miraculous from our daily lives.

Every day with God should be amazing and extraordinary. Even the mundane can become stunning in the presence of the Lord.

Let us not get too familiar with the presence of God. Remain in awe.

When we seek only miracles, we get only miracles. When we seek God, we get healed and transformed not just physically. When we focus on material things, we do get those things. But when we focus on God, we get so much more than what we need.

God SEES beauty in frailty

I was a fragile broken thing when God found me and I am amazed at how He could see past my frailty into my beauty.

2 Corinthians 4:6-7 NLT
"For God, who said, 'Let light shine out of darkness,' made His light shine in our hearts to give us the light of the knowledge of God's glory displayed in the face of Christ. We now have this light shining in our hearts, but we ourselves are like fragile clay jars containing this great treasure. This makes it clear that our great power is from God, not from ourselves."

GOD RESTORES US TO GREATER VALUE AND PURPOSE

I have yet to meet someone who has not been broken in any way.

Yet it seems that our frailty provides more opportunities for us to be restored into something greater.

When we were in Japan, my eldest son, Abdiel, was searching for old broken pottery. The more broken they were, the happier he was. But they turned out to be too expensive and unaffordable for us.

It was such a paradox that the newer, unbroken tea pots and mugs were way cheaper.

He explained to me the art of *Kintsugi.*

Wikipedia defines *kintsugi* as "to repair with gold.""

Wikipedia also states that:

> *"Kintsugi is the Japanese art of repairing broken pottery with lacquer dusted or mixed with powdered gold, silver, or platinum, a method similar to the maki-e technique. As a philosophy it treats breakage and repair as part of the history of an object, rather than something to disguise.*
>
> *"Kintsugi is the general concept of highlighting or emphasizing imperfections, visualizing mends and seams as additive or an area to celebrate or focus on rather than as absence or missing pieces.*
>
> *"As a philosophy kintsugi can be seen to have similarities to the Japanese philosophy of wabi-sabi, an embracing of the flawed or imperfect. Japanese aesthetics values marks of wear by the use of an object. This can be seen as a rationale for keeping an object around even after it has broken and as a justification of kintsugi itself, highlighting the cracks and repairs as simply an event in the life of an object rather than allowing its service to end at the time of its damage or breakage."[5]*

Wow! That sounds like us in the hands of the Greatest Potter!

I cannot remember who preached this, but he said: *"We go through hardship and trials because God sets us up to be rewarded."*

How could you reward someone who has not overcome hardships?

A warrior is hardly a victor if he has not won a battle.

James 1:2-3 NLT says *"Dear brothers and sisters, when troubles of any kind come your way, consider it an opportunity for great joy. For you know that when your faith is tested, your endurance has a chance to grow."*

The King James version is even better: *"Count it all joy…"*

It is so amazing that our value in the Lord is not measured by our form and services. We are loved and cherished simply because we are His children.

---

5 Wikipedia. Kintsugi. 2008 August (https://en.wikipedia.org/wiki/Kintsugi)

What is even more mind-blowing is, despite our brokenness and unworthiness, the blood of Jesus repaired our cracks and missing pieces to perfection and utmost value.

Grace is the Christian equivalent of *kintsugi* – just way more excellent.

Let me continue what was said in 2 Corinthians 4:

> *"We are hard pressed on every side, but not crushed; perplexed, but not in despair; persecuted, but not abandoned; struck down, but not destroyed. We always carry around in our body the death of Jesus, so that the life of Jesus may also be revealed in our body. For we who are alive are always being given over to death for Jesus' sake, so that his life may also be revealed in our mortal body. So then, death is at work in us, but life is at work in you."*

Our brokenness is *not* a hindrance to greatness.

When we run after God, we seek the Great Restorer. And God restores us to *greater* value and purpose.

If *Kintsugi* patches up every broken part with gold, a precious element that lasts forever, our God puts us together by something even more precious than gold. Colossians 1:17 says that Jesus *"holds us together."*

When I understood the value of being broken, I stopped using the word "problem" and substituted it with the word *"challenges."* Every *challenge* we encounter is simply a "prelude to victory."

As Christians, who have experienced *Kintsugi* from the Lord; we should become channels of *Kintsugi* for others.

The greatest restoration from our frailty is becoming a bearer of God's presence. We could become masters of forgiving and lead broken people to be repaired and remolded in the hands of God.

As mended pots that have become more valuable, we have the privilege to also increase the value of people around us through God's love and grace.

Instead of wishing the difficult people to vanish from our lives, let us pray that we would be a balm of healing and transformation. Our brokenness produces an empathy in us that turn us into people who are first to love and last to judge.

Our brokenness does not have to be chains that weigh us down, they can become our battle scars that are worn like medals – proof of God's amazing restorative power.

We are God's *Kintsugi*.

Kintsugi bowl [6]

[6] Amazing.zone. Kintsugi, cracks are beautiful. 2020 April 12 (https://amazing.zone/fotosblog/max/kintsugi-min.jpg)

THE MODEL

"Charm is deceptive, and beauty is fleeting; but a woman who fears the LORD *is to be praised."* **Proverbs 31:30 NIV**

This was written to encourage my dear sisters and to expand the wisdom of my brothers in Christ.

When I was young, I was the tallest Filipina in the area where we lived – 168 cm. I used to have porcelain skin and I was slim.

A lot of people urged me to be a fashion model.

Personally, that idea was impossible because I was incredibly clumsy. Oh, I have a thousand stories of going home bleeding from tumbles and falls.

I never thought I would ever be a model.

But miracles happen every day, don't they?

I look at myself and see all my faults and incapacities.

However, God has been standing nearby all my life beckoning me to come to Him. He is able to do the best makeover in my life. He is the great designer and I can choose to put on and show off His designs – of love, patience, kindness, faithfulness and compassion.

As it was stated in 2 Corinthians 3:2, *"you are like letters that are known and read by everyone."*

THIS MODEL IS UPGRADABLE

Did you know that when companies launch a new gadget, they are already getting ready with the next better model.

It is so hard to keep up with all the new things and technologies coming out. People go crazy over a new release, and yet the creators have already invented a better one.

It is precisely the same with God.

God is the great Creator who can reinvent and re-create you every single day.

While you and other people are still in amazement at how God has transformed you, "Thank You, Lord, for saving me," He is already saying "Wait till you see the next upgraded you!"

It reminds me of how the angel addressed Gideon as a mighty warrior even before he went to battle (Judges 6:12).

God is not finished with you and me. When you model for God, He prepares lines of designs for you for different, exciting upcoming seasons.

Allow me to cite models in this amazing Christian story – the women mentioned in Jesus' genealogy in the first chapter of Matthew.

What an honor God gave women to be included in that Hall of Fame.

TAMAR
Matthew 1:3; Genesis 38

Tamar was the wife of Er, Judah's first son, who died. She was then married off to Onan, who also died.

Hence, Judah refused to marry her off to his youngest son, Shelah because in his mind, his daughter-in-law couldn't bear a son and both his sons (her husbands) died – so she must be cursed.

Have you ever felt being cursed? You cannot do anything right. You feel you have nothing to offer. You are useless, therefore worthless.

Well, Tamar wanted so much to be fruitful and to bring forth a rightful heir to Judah. Her motives were so right but her method was so wrong. She had to cover herself with a veil and hide her true identity to achieve this.

When Judah's wife died and he had overcome his grief, Tamar disguised herself as a prostitute to sleep with him. Despite her deception, God saw the sincerity of her heart, forgave her and blessed her with two sons. To one, came the line of King David and Jesus.

HAIR

Your hair can be your glory…or your veil.

Have you ever used your hair to cover your face feeling incompetent and lacking in so many ways? The grace of God combs through your veil to reveal who you really are, and to make you fruitful.

THIS MODEL IS UPGRADABLE

The greatest gift of every woman is motherhood.

You do not need to grow big for nine months and go through the physical anguish of giving birth to exercise your gift of motherhood. You could carry a baby in your heart. You could give birth to a new life through sacrifices and love, and ultimately raise up a child in patience and affection.

Motherhood is so much more than just pushing out in pain. It is a long process of nurturing children, whether physical or spiritual, the people that God brings within your reach.

When you open your arms to care for teenagers hungry for love, when you patiently pray for someone, when you faithfully walk with another woman to let them know Jesus, when you disciple others to grow and mature spiritually – that is motherhood.

The world is hungry for mothers who would carry them, put their arms around them and guide them to grow. As a woman, you are very gifted to do that.

RAHAB

Matthew 1:5, Joshua 2 and 6

Rahab was a prostitute and she knew her lifestyle directly hurt and insulted the nature of God.

But when she came face to face with the love of God through a nation. She took the opportunity to allow God to change her.

She must have been so ashamed of who she was. I believe though, that there was a community of women in Israel who made this woman feel accepted, for her to turn to and serve their God.

Have you ever wished to go back and change things in your past? I wish I could tell you that as a pastor's wife, I am perfect. But I am not. I forget important appointments. I fail to respond to emails. Sometimes I am tempted to tell a lie because it is too embarrassing or too painful to tell the truth.

I have disappointed people.

I took on loads, I wasn't equipped to carry alone. I do get tired and become irritable.

I also have a past like everyone else and I have done things I am not very proud of.

I am in the same boat, needing God's grace to forge a new identity.

FACE

The blood of Jesus covers your sins and blemishes so He can present you blameless before God. It has extreme full coverage and it lasts forever even, in extreme heat.

I know because I have been applying the blood of Jesus in my life.

Whenever I'm afraid, the blood of Jesus gives me courage.

When there is illness, the blood of Jesus takes care of that. I apply the blood of Jesus in every situation of my life and it works.

From the very first 24 hours of applying the blood of Jesus I already saw a visible difference.

Today, after more than 30 years of applying the blood of Jesus in my life, others see a visible difference.

"You look great Mildred. What's your secret?" The blood of Jesus.

As you continuously apply the Blood of Jesus, it will regenerate and renew you. It exfoliates your "old self" and brings out the "new you" over and over and over again.

And you may apply it lavishly.

THIS MODEL IS UPGRADABLE.

There is no sin and mistake you have ever done that does not melt or is completely cleansed by the blood of the Lamb.

Your past does *not* create your identity. God does.

In fact, even your brokenness can become precious elements that help you fulfill your destiny and purpose.

It is *not* time that heals, it is God Who does.

RUTH

Matthew 1:5, and The Book of Ruth

Ruth was from the race of Moab, a people who were stubborn, disrespectful, idolaters, immoral and rebellious. They were cursed never to enter into the presence of the Lord even to the tenth generation – about 400 years (Deuteronomy 23:3).

Yet through the influence of her mother-in-law, Naomi – Ruth chose to turn to God. Ruth declared, "Your people shall be my people, and your God, my God."

All women would be wise to model after that kind of mother-in-law; and all the men would say, "Amen."

CLOTHES

The mercy of God took away your filthy garments and clothed you in righteousness, worthy to come before the presence of God. He took away your shabby character and dressed you in dignity, because you are precious.

You are the model of who God is.

Wear His character and walk on the streets for everyone to see His magnificent designs.

Without His glory adorning you, you are nothing.

Carry His name. Show off His marvelous works. Jesus shielded your nakedness with His blood so He can present you blameless and holy.

When you choose to wear God's designs, you will not be put to shame. When you choose love over hate, it will transform you into a joyful person. When you put on God's creations, you will not cower in fear. His wisdom gets you very far and you are able to do more than what you ever dreamed of, not because of who you are but because of who He is.

THIS MODEL IS UPGRADABLE

You may carry the DNA of a sinful nation or a family. But the curse of sin stops when you choose to let the blood of Jesus wash over you.

He transforms your DNA into His and you become a perfect model of His designs – faithfulness, obedience, love, compassion.

If you want to see your nation and family bow before God, be intentional to take steps to trend the fashion and style of a "real life" in God.

Be the righteous influence that speaks life to your family and nation, who puts an end to injustice, and who restores hope to people whose lineage has been tarnished by sin.

BATHSHEBA

Matthew 1:6; 2 Samuel 11

Bathsheba was a good woman. But she allowed a man – King David – to trample her principles.

She became an adulteress because she was fearful and weak. She couldn't say no to what she knew was wrong!

The Bible tells us that she mourned the death of her husband. She loved him. She was faithful but she allowed fear to overcome her moralities. She must have felt weary, fighting the advances of King David toward her and it became easier to yield than to stand her ground.

SHOES

Though your knees become feeble, He will renew your strength.

The joy of the Lord is your strength. You can walk with your head held high in the footsteps of God. How lovely are the feet of them who bring good news.

In whatever kind of shoes, you are comfortable in, stand strong in the righteousness of God.

THIS MODEL IS UPGRADABLE

Have you ever felt tired, weary and weak despite knowing the truth about God? It seems as though there were no more fight left in you.

When you put your trust in the Lord, He will fight the battle for you. You might fall many times, but you will never be utterly defeated. The Lord forgave Bathsheba and gave her a son, Solomon, who became one of the greatest kings of Israel.

MARY
Matthew 1 – 2, Luke 1 – 2,

Mary was the most righteous among the women in this list.

Her life shone so brightly for God that an entire chapter was written about her even in the Quran – Maryam.

Her influence went beyond her race and nation. This is who you look forward to, an upgraded model, that is still upgradable.

She was a woman who constantly acknowledged that she was a sinner who needed a Savior and who constantly humbled herself before God.

When the angel told her that she would be carrying God's Son through the power of the Holy Spirit, she did not hesitate to say *"Behold, I am the servant of the Lord; let it be to me according to your word."* (Luke 1:38 ESV)

There was uncertainty in her situation. She was a young woman who was already engaged to Joseph. So for her to be found pregnant was not *just* shameful but it *could* cost her her life!

People would think she was crazy, if she went around saying that she was pregnant with God's child. She was in a dark and unfamiliar zone.

EARINGS, NECKLACE, BANGLES

The Lord is the light in your darkness. He will shine through you. He shares His glory with you. He said He will make you shine like the noonday sun, like the stars in a dark night.

THIS MODEL IS UPGRADABLE

Mary was an ordinary woman with an extraordinary faith.

Darkness makes one blind. In the uncertainty of her future she chose to let God be her eyes.

God can use you mightily in your simplicity. No one can judge the greatness of your service by how popular and how big it is. Only God knows the faithful heart that desires to serve Him in the best way it can.

When you invite your neighbor to have coffee with you so you can be an extension of God's love to them, when you sacrifice time to see one woman know more of God, when everything you do is for the purpose of bringing Jesus in the lives of people – that is honorable.

Your radiance liberates others to shine with you.

It is not whether you are tall, slim, talented or glamorous that makes you valuable and beautiful. The Bible is your mirror. It tells you who you really are and what you are truly worth.

When you ask, "Who is the fairest of them all?" God responds, "It is you, my child, for I have fearfully and wonderfully made you." You are unique in all the earth. God has endowed everyone with something distinctive to give.

When you are around other models, it gets even better. Together you form a powerhouse of gifts and talents that the world needs to experience.

God does not expect you to do great wonders on visible platforms. If you can invite a fellow mother to church, or start a small group in your home or join forces with other women for the purpose of restoring dignity to women through the grace and love of God, that's already amazing.

IF YOU CAN ONLY SEE WHAT GOD SEES IN YOU!

"Beauty is in the eye of the beholder."

However, what other standards can compete with the perfect eyes of a perfect God? Your beauty is not your own, it comes from your great Designer, that is why you cannot even boast of it. It keeps you humble.

When your lives are completely in the Master's hands, it can be transformed into the loveliest creature on earth that shines, gives compassion, gives value to others and just a delight to be with.

You are a model. And God is Who makes you beautiful.

2nd Row, Jonathan, Gemma, Emmanuel, Raymond, Mildred, Abdiel
1st Row, Jennifer, Papa Solomon, Mama Virginia, Andrew

MILDRED BORBON OSIAS

Mildred Osias has started and co-pastored FCC churches in Europe with her husband, Raymond, since 1998 (www.fccc-family.com).

She was a Registered Nutritionist-Dietician, who graduated from the University of the Philippines (U.P.) in Diliman.

She responded to God's call to full-time ministry in 1987 and finished a Theology degree from Bethel Bible College. She later went back to U.P. to pursue MBA.

She has a passion for discipleship and has authored most of the discipleship materials being used in their churches. She has also been a conference speaker for several years.

Her passion is teaching and discipleship and her missions experience is quite extensive, from Asia and in Europe. She considers being a small group (Life Group) leader and mentor, without a break for 35 years, her most significant contribution in ministry.

CHAPTER 7

DESIGNED TO LOVE, TRUST AND SERVE THE MASTER

By Raymond Osias

WHY WOULD A LOVING GOD ALLOW EVIL?

If God is sovereign, and He is loving and all powerful, why would He allow evil, pain and suffering?

You are probably having some difficulty getting convincing answers to this question – like I used to.

This question can only be accurately answered by God.

Therefore, any attempt to answer this question can either be by presumption or by God's revelation.

I believe though, that we can find enough clues in the Bible to deduce an answer.

Based on the Bible, and knowing what happened in the past and what will happen in the future, studying and researching will give us satisfying answers.

The difficulty in answering this question lies heavily on the prevalence of evil around the world. A lot of people cannot accept the existence of God and evil at the same time.

In their book "Handbook of Christian Apologetics" Peter Kreeft and Ronald K. Tacelli explain that the difficulty can be summed up by what *seems* to be contradictions between the following four propositions:

1.   God exists
2.   God is all good
3.   God is all-powerful; and
4.   Evil exists

They say that if we accept that God exists and is completely good and all-powerful, then evil cannot exist. If we accept that God exists, is all good and that evil exists, then God is not all-powerful, because He couldn't stop evil. If God exists and is all-powerful and yet evil exists, then God must not be completely good, because He is allowing evil to exist.

But, I think they are missing some of the important truths about God.

It is true that God is completely good and all-powerful, but He is also all-knowing, righteous, just and wise. In fact, the Bible said that God's foolishness is wiser than the wisdom of man. (1 Corinthians 1:25)

The prophet Jeremiah quoted God saying:

"Thus, says the LORD: 'Let not the wise man glory in his wisdom, Let not the mighty man glory in his might, Nor let the rich man glory in his riches; But let him who glories glory in this, That he understands and knows Me, That I am the LORD, exercising lovingkindness, judgment, and righteousness in the earth. For in these I delight,' says the LORD."
Jeremiah 9:23-24 (NKJV)

The passage clearly tells us that God delights in making Himself known and understood by man. He delights to make Himself known as the God of love, justice and righteousness, and definitely to be known for who He really is.

Since we cannot deny the truth that God is love, just and righteous, completely good, all-knowing, and all-powerful we are only left to accept that God in all His wisdom has allowed and has been allowing evil to exist.

What could be the reason then?

We all can agree that nothing happens without God's permission because He knows all things and He can do all things. That is why evil exists – because God is allowing it, which I believe will only be temporary.

Evil is not eternal and I am sure God will not allow it to stay forever according to the Scriptures – at least in His Kingdom and for the rest of eternity.

EVIL, A RESULT OF DISOBEDIENCE TO GOD

One of the best gifts of God to human beings and to all the angels next to life is their freedom to obey God, His will and His purpose – or to disobey God, follow their own ways and will.

Intelligent beings like man and angels were given the abilities to know right and wrong, and the freedom to decide for themselves.

Since God is perfectly good, righteous and holy, everything contrary to that and His nature is considered evil.

I don't think it was a coincidence that the word "evil" is spelled exactly the opposite of the word "live" because logically speaking, to choose evil is to give up life and God who is the source of life.

When angels and man chose to disobey God, they chose as well to become the enemies of God. It leaves them with only one option and tendency - to be the exact opposite of God's good and perfect nature.

No creature of God can be disobedient and remain good, because God's will and decisions are always coming from His goodness, righteousness, love and wisdom. To disobey God therefore, is to cut oneself from God's direction, guidance and will.

Obedience on the other hand leads to a life of harmony, order and peace with God.

When Satan and a third of the angels chose to follow their own will and ways, they became the enemies of God – and they gave birth to evil.

Ever since then they have been trying to bring the whole human race down with them, but Jesus stopped them.

REASONS FOR ALLOWING EVIL

TO REVEAL AND EXPOSE EVIL

God is truth. He does not delight in anything false or in whitewashed tombs. No matter how ugly and unpleasant it may look He desires truth in everything.

In fact, the Bible is not only full of good stories and triumphs of His chosen people, but it is also full of their failures, mistakes and ugliness.

Evil is something that God does not want to hide. By temporarily allowing evil to exist, God is revealing to all His creatures the true image of evil and how horribly evil, evil really is.

He wants to expose the ugliness of evil and how cruel, hellish and horrific it is. He wants to show His creatures how one simple disobedience could lead to the worst evil.

If God just gave His creatures some kind of pre-programmed knowledge and information about evil, they would only get the *theory* about it.

This is why God has allowed evil to exist, so it would be exposed and so everyone would know what evil really is. Otherwise evil would just be hidden inside a black hole.

By allowing evil to exist, God can end the ignorance and the eternal tendency of His creatures to rebel against Him.

On the other hand, if God never allowed evil to exist, none of His creatures would ever know and understand how a loving God would judge and condemn evil.

No one would understand what God's justice, love and righteousness really means if someone chooses to disobey Him. It would forever be something left unanswered and unknown to all of God's creatures.

Temporarily allowing evil will in the end destroy humans' and angels' lack of knowledge and experience with regards to how God responds to evil – which we already know that God the Father would have to send His only Son and allow Him to suffer to save mankind.

Allowing evil will completely destroy rebellion in the end, not just because God is just but also because everybody will know that there is nothing good whatsoever with evil.

God will definitely put an end to evil one day but He couldn't end something that had never even started.

After He has allowed evil to exist for some time, His creatures will, in the end, realized how terrible evil is and will all agree with God that it should not be allowed to continue to exist.

Unless God allows it to exist for a while, none of His creatures would realize its true image, effects, and the reasons why it should be eradicated forever.

DEEPER KNOWLEDGE OF GOD, HIS GOODNESS AND LOVE

My youngest son Andrew also had the difficulty of accepting the fact that God had allowed evil.

In one of our long discussions, he purported that God should have just pre-educated man about His nature and everything to know about evil, sparing the universe from all the troubles and sparing Jesus from sufferings and from dying on the cross.

I had to explain to him that if none of these happened, then everything we would know about God and His nature would simply be theories…without any bearing, because they would merely be information and words without substance.

What I find to be the most significant revelation coming from allowing evil to exist for a while is that all creation witnesses, experiences and learns how deep, great and amazing the love of God is for His creatures!

Otherwise our knowledge and experience of God's love would just be limited to His provisions, protections and eternal fellowship with Him, since no creature would have disobeyed nor sinned against Him.

We would never know that God's love can take precedence over His glory which was revealed to us when Jesus left His glory in heaven, came in a limited and fragile human body, subjected Himself to human injustice and cruelty, and allowed evil to have its own way over His human life – confronting God's infinite love.

Jesus, who created everything including angels, was found obedient to the Father to the point of death, humiliating Satan and his followers when Jesus humbled and made Himself a little lower than Satan and his minions, and yet obeyed the Father in everything – even in sufferings and death.

The way God responded, dealt with and destroyed evil brought a deeper and complete knowledge of God's character and nature. Evil revealed God's justice, righteousness, love and goodness in its depth that could never have been possible if evil had remained a secret.

Much of God's character and nature could never be known to man and the angels if evil and disobedience were never allowed by God.

We would never know the love that Jesus demonstrated on the cross because there would be no need for Him to save mankind.

We would never have known mercy since no one would've needed it; we would never have known justice because nobody would've disobeyed; we would never have known forgiveness since nobody would have sinned, and we would never have known God's amazing grace the way we do now.

Perhaps our understanding of grace would've only been limited to God's generous gifts and provisions, but never as amazing as when Jesus took our penalties and death. We would never know what complete goodness means without the stark contrast of the face of evil.

EVIL THE PRICE OF FREEWILL

God allowed evil as a consequence of giving His creatures the gift of *free will*.

Obedience would not really be obedience unless there is an option to disobey. Submission would not really be submission unless there is an option to rebel. And evil, its pain and consequences have been the most costly price that God and His creatures have had to pay.

God in His wisdom had to allow it because it will bring eternal and infinitely remarkable results in the end.

As God gave Adam and Eve two choices – to obey or to disobey, to submit or to rebel, He also gave everyone the same freedom but not without consequences.

In the end we will all know the consequences of evil, and that they only lead to the greatest cost which Jesus had to pay.

But the greatest love of all was demonstrated right at the face of the greatest evil of all when Jesus our Creator surrendered Himself to the works of evil so that He could impute to man His righteousness, love and forgiveness.

Because of man's freedom to choose, Jesus had to humble Himself and be confined in a human body, insulted, mocked, falsely accused, falsely judged, tortured, murdered and rejected by His own creatures – all because He wants to keep us all from evil, and win our choice to live in trust and obedience to God.

The price for giving God's creatures the freedom of choice was so costly, but it is also the most rewarding.

IN THE END

God will cleanse His kingdom from sin, rebellion, pride, envy, jealousy, selfishness, and from everything contrary to His nature. God intends to bring His eternal righteousness, love, joy, peace, kindness, goodness and all His great character and all the beauty of His nature to all His creatures.

After God has allowed evil to exist for a while – after evil is exposed and has revealed its true image, judged and condemned…after it has revealed God's true character and nature in response to evil, then *no creature* of God will ever wonder, question or challenge God's will, purpose and works forever.

Everyone will know God's love, justice and righteousness. Everyone can choose to love, serve and obey God with complete knowledge of God's nature, His character and holiness.

Everyone will love God not as blind lovers. Everyone will serve God not merely as blind servants. Everyone will follow God not with blind obedience, but willingly, lovingly, gratefully, and voluntarily with all their hearts, soul, mind and strength.

Oh! What a wonderful heaven and God's kingdom it will be! I want to be there. Do you want to be there?

You were divinely designed to be there.

God wants you there.

Make sure you will be there.

THE PERFECT STORM IN THE FACE OF THE PERFECT FAITH

"One day Jesus said to his disciples, 'Let's cross to the other side of the lake.' So they got into a boat and started out. As they sailed across, Jesus settled down for a nap. But soon a fierce storm came down on the lake. The boat was filling with water, and they were in real danger. The disciples went and woke him up, shouting, 'Master, Master, we're going to drown!'

"When Jesus woke up, he rebuked the wind and the raging waves. The storm stopped and all was calm! Then he asked them, 'Where is your faith?' The disciples were terrified and amazed. 'Who is this man? they asked each other. 'When he gives a command, even the wind and waves obey him!'"
Luke 8:22-25 (NLT)

I love this story because I can relate it to all our challenges in life.

In the Philippines, storms are a regular part of life. Storms used to be very unpredictable before modern technology.

However, for many years now, storms can be forecasted. But squalls are still difficult to forecast since they normally cover a smaller area. They come and leave so quickly with fierce winds and heavy rains or snow.

What Jesus and His disciples encountered in the passage was a squall, because there was no sign of it when they started out.

When the disciples met the squall or the storm, they were caught unprepared, just like some of the big challenges we sometimes encounter.

These trials and challenges come barging in, without politely knocking at the door. And they create so much damage on their way out!

The storm that Jesus and his disciples met was not just an ordinary one, it was a perfect storm that only a perfect faith could calm down.

This was why the disciples were so frightened and completely *amazed* when they witnessed how Jesus stopped the storm.

What could have they learned from the experience?

JESUS' IDEA IS HIS ASSURANCE.

According to the story, it was Jesus' idea to cross the lake. Because it was His idea, it meant that He would make sure they would make it to the other side. He would be responsible to keep the safety of every one of them.

In the end, they all made it to the other side, even though the unexpected perfect storm showed up.

You see, God impresses ideas on you.

Sometimes, you know for sure that you heard from Him.

At times, it seems though, that a kind of perfect storm is making it difficult to achieve.

If you really heard from God, then you can be sure He will do His part to help you accomplish it.

Now if what you heard is unbiblical or against the principles of God, then it is definitely *not* from God.

When I prayed for Mildred, my wife, before I proposed to her in 1992, I combined my ability to hear from God and my own preferences to know for sure that she would be the best partner I would like to spend my whole life with.

Therefore, every time we went through challenges in our marriage, I always approached God and reminded Him that it was His idea. He had reassured me, time and again, that it was and it would always be His.

So, knowing that it was God's idea, we were able to weather challenges by His grace, even those trials that seemed like perfect storms.

Whatever it is that God called you to do, you can be sure that He will see you through. Do not focus too much on the storm, but rather go to God in prayer so He can remind you that it was His idea and that He is with you.

PERFECT NAP IN THE PERFECT STORM

"As they sailed across, Jesus settled down for a nap. But soon a fierce storm came down on the lake. The boat was filling with water, and they were in real danger." Luke 8:23 (NLT).

Do you know anyone who could sleep so deeply in the middle of a storm?

Well, Jesus was one of them. He had no problem sleeping. That was why His brain was efficiently functioning whenever He was awake. He took power naps whenever He needed one.

When the disciples were struggling to keep the boat afloat and were in danger, Jesus was sleeping like a log!

I call it the *"perfect nap"* because only a perfect storm could be the perfect scene for a *perfect nap*. He wasn't just pretending to be asleep. He wasn't just testing to see if His disciples were good enough to bring the boat to shore. No, He was genuinely asleep.

If this was the devil's attack, then the enemy found the perfect time to shake the disciples – while Jesus was asleep. The devil did not know what Jesus would do to the storm. He took the chance. Perhaps the devil didn't want Jesus to get to the other side because he had a stronghold there – a man possessed by many demons.

I wonder how many people can sleep in the middle of the storm, probably not many.

It is difficult to sleep when we are facing a big problem especially when it looks like a perfect storm.

The storms of life can come in many different shapes and sizes. It may appear as a relational issue, a big financial challenge requiring you to raise a huge amount of money, sickness and pain that never seem to get healed, a corona virus that locks you down, or any kind of very challenging situation that you don't have a clue how to deal with.

Whatever storms you may be facing right now, or might be facing in the future, remember that Jesus might just be "sleeping over it," waiting for you to call upon Him and wake Him up.

When you do not pray to ask God for help, you are simply telling Him you *can* handle it all by yourself.

Although Jesus was there together with His disciples on the boat, they had to cry out and wake Him up.

The boat could have been dashed and Jesus awoken by the crash. Jesus could have been pulling each disciple out from the water. Imagine Him saying, *"Why didn't you wake me up? Now, we won't eat for some days because we have to pay for the boat."*

Storms are *meant* for us to **call upon God** and experience His power to calm the seas.

Call on Jesus before things get worse. In fact, we should always pray for protection. *"Lead us not into temptation, but deliver us from evil"* can be part of our daily prayer to God. (Matthew 6:13 ESV)

Only a *perfect storm* can bring *perfect sleep* and once you've experienced how God calms a perfect storm, no storm can take your sleep away.

PERFECT STORM IN THE FACE OF THE PERFECT FAITH

"When Jesus woke up, he rebuked the wind and the raging waves.

"Suddenly the storm stopped and all was calm! Then he asked them, 'Where is your faith?' The disciples were terrified and amazed. 'Who is this man? they asked each other. When he gives a command, even the wind and waves obey him!'" Luke 8:24b-25 (NLT)

Before Jesus rebuked the storm, no one had ever done it.

Jesus was the original. If Jesus did not know He had authority to rebuke the winds and the storm, He could have made the boat fly or called for angels to escort them to the shore, blocking the winds and the waves.

But it does not really matter how Jesus could have done it. The point is, Jesus was more interested in building the trust and the faith of His disciples, because only a *perfect storm* can build a *perfect faith*.

They saw *perfect faith* in action before their eyes and that was astonishing and unforgettable, because after Jesus rebuked the storm and the waves, you can imagine how the disciples would've looked like if they took a selfie afterwards.

Do you know what the experience did to them?

"Who is this?", they asked. He was sleeping – unbothered.

Then, they saw the same God who created the sun, moon, stars and the universe – stop the perfect storm. The encounter definitely changed their lives and they never forgot what happened there.

WHAT HAVE WE LEARNED

What storm are you facing today?

Whatever storm you are facing, I am sure, it is not intended to destroy the boat you are on, or to stop you from getting to where Jesus is leading you.

His idea is your assurance that you will get to where you should be. Just go to Him for help and He will give you peace – assuring you that He heard you and that He will keep His words.

If you think it's a perfect storm...it calls for a perfect faith.

Jesus asked His disciples after He rebuked the storm, *"Where is your faith?"*

Trust Him, He who is able to sleep in the middle of the perfect storm, because no perfect storm can stand against the perfect faith.

Remember that you were divinely designed to weather all kinds of storms...even the most perfect storm – because Jesus is with you.

SERVING A GREATER PURPOSE

Our lives can only be as meaningful as our sense of purpose.

Mark Twain said, *"The two most important days in your life are the day you are born and the day you find out why."*

If we do not know our purpose in life, we merely exist.

And until we find our purpose, nothing in life will really satisfy.

We were created to live life with a purpose.

One of the people I admire in the Bible is the apostle Paul because he knew exactly what he wanted to accomplish in life and was so passionate about it.

He was an extremely ambitious person. When he laid out all his credentials in Philippians 3:4-6, it gives us a clear understanding of what he was committed to and focused in accomplishing in life.

Nothing *could* convince him to change the direction of his life, *until* he met Jesus, and discovered that there was something greater than what he thought was already the best.

His encounter with Jesus radically changed his life.

He left *everything* behind and started serving a greater purpose with even more passion and determination.

NOTHING GREATER THAN SERVING THE PURPOSES OF GOD

Whatever purpose we are serving, I believe there will never be anything better than serving the purposes of God.

God is our Maker and He knows all of us. He knows what is best for us and what is best for the whole universe.

Rabbi Noah Weinberg once said, *"Until you know what you are willing to die for, you have not yet begun to live."* Most people believe that their sense of purpose is worth dying for. But to serve something really worth dying for, definitely would be the greatest.

The apostle Paul and all the other apostles lived and died serving their greatest purpose.

Paul said it himself in Acts 20:24 (NIV) when he was on his way to Jerusalem expecting persecution: *"However, I consider my life worth nothing to me, if only I may finish the race and complete the task the Lord Jesus has given me — the task of testifying to the gospel of God's grace."*

And we know that he ultimately died serving his greatest purpose.

I do not know if you already found the greater purpose you are willing to die for, or if you already found your purpose in life.

But unless you have a special call from God, the way God designed you will be His initial purpose for you. It means that the gifts, talents, skills and abilities that God has given you – are the starting points by which you can serve God's purposes.

And when you use them for God's glory, you will not only serve God's purposes, but you will also find your abilities growing in quality and capacity.

King David *"had* **served the purposes of God** *in his own generation"* before he died according to Acts 13:36-37 NASB.

We are all called to serve God's purposes in our generation – whether in a big or a small way, as long as we occupy our own spot in the puzzle of God's plan and design for the whole universe, we will still be serving our greater purpose.

If you have not discovered yours yet, just keep on seeking while serving Him with what you temporarily believe as your purpose and He will lead you there.

"The meaning of life is to find your gift; the purpose of life is to give it away."
~Pablo Picasso

NOTHING GREATER THAN HELPING SOMEONE GET SAVED.

"I am not ashamed of the gospel, because it is the power of God for the salvation of everyone who believes: first for the Jew, then for the Gentile."
Romans 1:16 (NIV)

The Apostle Paul gave his life for the preaching of the gospel and even changed the way he treated others just to win them to the faith.

He wrote, *"Though I am free and belong to no man, I make myself a slave to everyone, to win as many as possible. To the Jews I became like a Jew, to win the Jews…"* 1 Corinthians 9:19-23 (NIV).

When my wife and I were in a big shopping mall in the Philippines several years ago, we had to separate ways because she had an appointment that was only for women, so I had to go home alone.

Because I was not so familiar with the place, I got lost looking for the exit that led to the public transportation area.

After going in circles for about 30 minutes, I got tired and decided to just take a cab. I hailed the first available cab as soon as I got out of a mall exit.

The driver was a bit talkative, so we instantly started a conversation talking about life and politics. After some time, I decided to ask him if he attended church, to which he admitted that he had not been doing so for a long while. He said he was not religious.

I asked him if he knew for sure that he would go to heaven when he died. He said 'no' and that he was not sure. So, I started sharing the gospel, the love of God and what Jesus did for him on the cross. He just listened attentively while driving.

Afterwards, I asked him if he wanted to be saved and to receive Jesus into his heart. He said 'yes!' So I led him to pray with me the sinner's invitation for Jesus to take over the helm of his life. He asked God to forgive his sins and he declared that he now believed Jesus died, was buried and rose again for him so that he could live a new life.

As soon as we were done praying, He immediately exclaimed loudly that he felt so replete. "I am full! I am full!", he excitedly said. He was so happy that he got saved!

We arrived at my destination. I shook his hand and paid him a little extra which made him even happier and thankful.

When I pondered on what happened, I realized that the 30 minutes I lost looking for the public transport was not a coincidence. The Lord appointed that time for me to meet the cab driver.

He was given the opportunity to hear the gospel and to get saved.

I smiled remembering how the cab driver was shouting after getting saved. Perhaps because of poverty, the only words he could muster to express what he felt was that his hunger had been completely satisfied. He definitely got spiritually filled.

What an unforgettable experience. There is nothing better than being able to help someone get saved.

NOTHING GREATER THAN HELPING OTHERS FULFILL GOD'S PURPOSES FOR THEIR LIVES

Jesus commissioned His disciples to disciple all nations before He went back to heaven as mentioned in Matthew 28:19-20 (NIV).

There is no better way to help someone discover God's purposes in their lives than through discipleship – making God known to them, helping them discover His will and learn His ways. Discipleship shapes the minds and the hearts of people for God.

Winston Churchill said, *"We make a living by what we get, but we make life by what we give."*

The best thing we can lead everyone to is eternal life in God through the gospel and discipleship. As we invest our time and energy in discipleship, we multiple the number of people who serve a greater purpose. Remember how the Apostle Paul invested his life in others by risking his own life for them in Acts 20:35-38 (NIV)?

A while back, we visited the U.S. Veterans Hospital in Quezon City, Philippines. It was part of our outreach program to pray for the sick and to share the gospel with patients.

As soon as we arrived at the place, everyone went straight to different rooms and started ministering to people.

I noticed a man lying on a hospital bed along the corridor while a nurse was attending to his needs. I went straight to the patient wondering why he was missed by everyone.

Then I noticed that the nurse was dripping some water into the mouth of the patient. I asked her what was wrong with him.

She said that the patient has not been eating for a month. He was already so thin and very weak. He did not have any relatives who came to visit and help. The nurses were spending so much time taking care of the patient.

I began talking to the patient, sharing the love of God and the gospel while the nurse was watching. At the end of the sharing, I asked him if he wanted to receive Jesus and give his life to Him through prayer. He said 'yes'. With what little energy he had left, he prayed after me for forgiveness and salvation.

After the prayer, I asked him if he still wanted me to read the Book of John for him. He declined and said that he was already tired and wanted to rest.

I left him with the nurse and went to the wards to minister to other patients.

I later went out to check on how the patient at the corridor was doing. To my surprise, I saw the nurse covering the head of the patient with a blanket. I approached and asked her what happened. She said that shortly after I talked to him, he passed away.

I realized that God kept him alive just until that moment someone could share the gospel with him! I was so happy that I did not miss him and that our church was at the right place and at the right time.

I'm sure I'll meet him again in heaven one day.

I don't know if you can find anything better than leading someone to Christ, and helping someone discover and fulfill God's purposes in their lives.

For me it is the best and the most eternally rewarding endeavor in life.

Do not let anything stop you from seeking, discovering and fulfilling God's greater purposes in your life, no matter how hard and challenging they may be.

You have been divinely designed for it, so go for it.

Let me end with a quote from Trent Shelton, *"God has a purpose in your life that is far greater than your pain. Don't let the struggle you are currently going through keep you from the blessings that God has for you."*

Left to Right: Raymond, his wife Mildred, Julie, Abdiel and Andrew

RAYMOND OSIAS

Raymond Osias has been married for 27 years and has two sons.

He has been a pastor in the Philippines since 1987. He came to Denmark in 1998, together with his family and wife, Mildred, to pioneer a Christian church, FCC in Copenhagen.

FCC has expanded to ten daughter and granddaughter churches in different major cities in Europe and two in the Philippines.

He is a graduate of Civil Engineering from the Far Eastern University and later finished a second degree in Theology at Bethel Bible College. He also attended a month-long leadership training in Haggai Institute in Singapore. You could read more about FCC at www.fccc-family.com.

CHAPTER 8

DIVINELY DESIGNED LIFE GOALS

By Pastor Enrique Sarthou and Agnes Sarthou, PhD.

LIFE GOALS FOR TRUE SUCCESS

By Enrique "Ricky" Sarthou

How many of you want to live a *long* life?

Are you sure you want to live a long life…regardless of your health condition?

How many of you want to live a *strong* life?

Great! But is that *all* there is to life?

You could live a *strong* life, but what if it is only one-third of the life span of everyone else?

How many of you would like to live a *long* and *strong* life?

Are you sure? Are you willing to live so long on this earth and all your friends are gone, and all the stuff you watch on TV you don't understand, and the music you hear doesn't make sense to you?

Well, of course we all have our desires about our lives, we want to live long, live strong.

Well, I'd like to share a few stories, a few are from people from the Bible, some are not, but I think we can learn things from them on how to live life.

Because there are things beyond our control, and in the end, a lot of it has to do with our *perspective* – living life the way God wants us to live.

The Story of Sam Berns

Sam Berns was afflicted with progeria.

Progeria is an extremely rare genetic disorder which causes rapid advance in aging, and throughout the world, there are only 250 living people who are afflicted with this disease.

Ironically, Sam's mother and father are both pediatric physicians. They are both accomplished pediatricians in the Boston medical world. And yet their son was born with progeria.

Sam had an amazing outlook in life – he achieved *almost everything* he wanted to achieve.

Though he only weighted 50 lbs., he won many awards in school, attended his school's homecoming dance and even played at the halftime of a game, with the school's marching band – using a very light strap and snare drum designed by his parents, himself and an engineer.

He loved LEGOs and built some amazing LEGO® structures. Sam Berns even appeared on a TEDxTalk and a TED Med Talk.

In one appearance, he shared his philosophy in life, *"I try not to waste time feeling bad for myself, because when I do, there's no room for happiness... I surround myself with people that I want to be with. And I keep moving forward."*

Sam Berns died in 2014 – he was only 17 years old.

Did he live a long life? Some say yes, some say no.

The expected life span for someone with progeria is 14, he was 17. So some say he beat the odds.

I believe he lived a *strong* life, because his life displayed strength that many other people without such a disease *fail to exhibit* in their own lives.

Do you know what the definition of TRUE SUCCESS is?

True success is...

To be all God wants you to be, and do all God wants you to do, and to one day hear Him say, *"Well done, good and faithful servant."*

And here are some "Life Goals for True Success"

1. Take care of your mind and body
2. Make every day count
3. Prioritize relationships – first with God, then with people

The Story of Abraham

Abraham was an amazing man.

In Genesis 15:5, God made an incredible promise to him, *"Look up into the sky and count the stars if you can. That's how many descendants you will have!"*

Isn't that an astounding promise?

Then Genesis 24:1 states: *"Abraham was now very old, and the Lord had blessed him **in every way**."* [bold font for emphasis only]

Would you like for other people to say that about you in the later years of your life – that you were *blessed in every way*?

I'd love to be blessed...and not just blessed, but to be blessed *in every aspect of life*.

Let us learn a little bit more about Abraham.

First of all, James 2:23 NIV states – *"And the Scripture was fulfilled that says, 'Abraham believed God, and it was credited to him as righteousness,' and he was called God's friend."*

You see, Abraham had a genuine relationship with God – it *wasn't* merely another religion, it was a deep and personal relationship.

And obviously Abraham had a relationship with his family members and a lot of other people because he was a wealthy person.

I also think he was in good physical condition – as the diet prescribed by God was a very healthy one.

Hebrews 11:8 NIV states *"By faith Abraham, when called to go to a place he would later receive as his inheritance, obeyed and went, even though he did not know where he was going."*

He was a man of faith. And the Bible does tell us that he had a certainty and a peace regarding the promises of God.

We're also told in Hebrews 11:9-10 *"By faith he made his home in the promised land like a stranger in a foreign country; he lived in tents, as did Isaac and Jacob, who were heirs with him of the same promise. For he was looking forward to the city with foundations, whose architect and builder is God.*

When Abraham walked his many years on this earth, he walked it in a strong, heartfelt relationship with his God.

He was not a perfect person, his earthly life was not perfect…but certainly his faith in God impacted the way he lived. It impacted his relationships, and other aspects of his life.

Most important of all, Abraham knew, that if a person has a relationship with God, the best is yet to come.

So he *didn't* mind leaving the comforts of his former homeland, and exploring what God had in store for him. Because as that verse says, he was *"looking forward to the city with foundations, whose architect and builder was God."*

The Story of Moses

Moses is another amazing guy, and we can infer some things from his life.

I can safely say that he was in excellent physical shape because in one chapter in the book of Exodus, you can count how many times Moses went up and down, up and down the mountain.

> Exodus 19:3 – *"Then Moses went up to God, and the Lord called to him from the mountain and said, 'this is what you are to say to the descendants of Jacob and what you are to tell the people of Israel'…"*

> 19:7-8 *"So Moses went back and summoned the elders of the people and set before them all the words the Lord had commanded him to speak. The people all responded together, 'we will do everything the Lord has said.'"*

So Moses brought their answer back to the Lord.

> 19:14 *"After Moses had gone down the mountain to the people, he consecrated them, and they washed their clothes."*

> 19:20 *"The Lord descended to the top of Mount Sinai and called Moses to the top of the mountain. So Moses went up…"*

> 19:25 *"So Moses went down to the people and told them."*

How many times did he go up and down?

I myself got tired from merely counting, so he must really have been in great shape. The Lord really made him exercise well.

Yet that is not the best part of Moses' life.

> Deuteronomy 34:5,7 – *"And Moses the servant of the Lord died there in Moab, as the Lord had said. Moses was a hundred and twenty years old when he died, yet his eyes were not weak nor his strength gone."*

Just to open with you, this is actually my prayer for myself and for my wife, that throughout our lives, with the number of years that God would give us, that our eyes would not dim, and our strength would not be gone.

Isn't that an excellent prayer?

Numbers 12:1 – reveals something about Moses' character, how he dealt with people, and his relationship with God

Verse 1 "Miriam and Aaron began to talk against Moses because of his Cushite wife, for he had married a Cushite."

Who were Miriam and Aaron? They were Moses's siblings. Sometimes the most challenging relationships in life are our closest relationships.

Let's look at the scenario.

At first, Miriam's and Aaron's issue against Moses was regarding his Cushite wife.

Then in Numbers 12:2-3 Miriam and Aaron speaking to Moses, *"Has the Lord spoken only through Moses?"* they said. "Hasn't he also spoken through us?" and the Lord heard this. (Now Moses was a very humble man, more humble than anyone else on the face of the earth.)

But look at how Moses responded,

It reminds us one of the secrets of healthy relationships is having humility in the heart, not thinking ourselves more highly than we should.

God took care of Moses, and Moses did not have to defend himself.

So what else can we learn about Moses?

Going back to Hebrews, just like what we read about Abraham, here in Hebrews 11:24-26 it says, By faith Moses, when he had grown up… chose to be mistreated along with the people of God rather than to enjoy the fleeting pleasures of sin.

Both Abraham's and Moses's perspectives about life were that *"God gave me this life, I am going to make the most of it. And the most important part, is my relationship with God, and because I have a relationship with Him, the best after this life is yet to come."*

Billy Graham died at an amazing age of 99, and this is what he said, *"Someday you will read or hear that Billy Graham is dead. Don't you believe a word of it. I shall be more alive than I am now. I will just have changed my address. I will have gone into the presence of God"*

So can we learn from the lives of these people we've discussed so far?

I think so. Are you inspired?

Let's go to another story.

This is two sets of footprints in the sand, but no people.

I'll explain to you why. I will tell you about my favorite characters in the bible, but not many people talk about him. His name is Enoch. If you go to Genesis chapter 5, you will see a long list of people, of men, and who their spouses were, and who the sons, and the sons of the sons were.

> Genesis 5:18-20 *"When Jared had lived 162 years, he became the father of Enoch. After he became the father of Enoch, Jared lived 800 years and had other sons and daughters. Altogether, Jared lived a total of 962 years, and then he died."*

Now for some of you, you might think, come on, that must be a typo – well let's put it this way, if the Bible says it, I believe it. And if we have a problem with it, when we see God we can ask Him. I will skip one generation.

> Genesis 5:21-24 – *"When Enoch had lived 65 years, he became the father of Methuselah. After he became the father of Methusela, Enoch walked faithfully with God 300 years and had other sons and daughters.*
>
> *Altogether, Enoch lived a total of 365 years. Enoch walked faithfully with God; then he was no more, because God took him away."*

Enoch's life was different, it was different in a few ways, one is rather than just saying he died, it said that God took him away.

Second is, it is only in his case, that we read that he walked faithfully with God, he had relationship with God.

And he also lived the shortest life, only 365 years. Is that long? Or short?

When the typically lifespan then was 800-900 years, 300+ years is not a long life. And yet, he walked faithfully with God. Amazing

Do you remember the movie "Chariots of Fire"?

It's a movie about a man named Eric Liddell. Eric was a Scottish athlete, a champion runner.

In 1924, Eric was supposed to run the 100 meter dash in the Paris Olympics, and it was scheduled on a Sunday.

Because of his commitment to God and his personal conviction based on the Bible to keep his Sabbath day, he told the Olympic officials that wouldn't run.

He could've decided to run, would've likely won the race, and then later have made an excuse such as: "Well, I didn't have a choice, it was out of my control."

Instead, he stuck to his convictions and honored God. He said he wouldn't run, and he didn't.

So the Olympic officials entered Eric in the 400 meter run instead.

And guess what! By God's grace, God honored Eric, such that he established a new Olympic world record in the 400 meter run!

Now why am I sharing about our brother in Christ – Eric Lidell?

Well, the year after the Olympics, he did what he thought God called him to do *after* completing his assignment to glorify the LORD, and *feel GOD's pleasure* whenever he used his God-given ability to run *fast* on the worldwide stage, with humility and conviction.

And that next assignment was to be a missionary to China.

So Eric went to Northern China and he gave his full life to serving God, and telling the Chinese people about Jesus.

When the Japanese occupation came, it was an awful time for the Chinese people. It also made life very difficult for Eric, and because of the dire living conditions, he became ill. He developed a brain tumor, and because there was no way for him to seek any kind of medical treatment, he died at the age of 43.

Eric did not live a long life…but his was a life lived well.

One of the people who survived him was a fellow inmate since some were incarcerated, like prisoners of war.

Anyway, this inmate who survived him shared a memory of Eric: *"Do you know one thing that Eric taught me? He taught me how to love my enemies. He taught me how to love the Japanese. He taught me how to forgive."*

Even though Eric's life was short, he had an amazing impact on the people around him.

The Story of Jesus

Now the best and most perfect example for us is Jesus.

Jesus is the best example of all when it comes to looking after Himself, His mind, His body, making every day count and focusing on His relationships – first with His heavenly Father, and then with His disciples…which includes you.

How do we know that He is the perfect example?

Well, the Bible tells us in Luke 2:52 – *"And Jesus grew in wisdom and stature, and in favor with God and man."*

Take care of your mind – what you think about fills you.

For people like Moses, for Abraham, for Eric – all of these people filled their minds and their hearts with the word of God.

And that is why in spite of challenges, and regardless of not knowing how long or short their lives would be, it filled them with a sense of purpose, a sense of peace, in spite of the trials that befell them.

But in the case of Jesus, we see the perfect example. He grew in wisdom and stature, and in favor with God and man. And rather than looking at a lot of verses that support this, I'd rather take it from a different angle by sharing this poetic essay with you.

It is called "One Solitary Life" based on the essay of Dr. James Allan Francis.

> "There was a man who was born in an obscure village, the child of peasant woman. He grew up in still another village where He worked in a carpenter shop until He was thirty. Then for three years He was an itinerant preacher.

> "He never wrote a book. He never held an office. He never had a family or owned a home. He never went to college. He never put his foot inside a big city. He never traveled two hundred miles from the place where he was born. He never did one of the things that usually accompany greatness. He had no credentials but himself. He had nothing to do with this world except the pure power of his divine nature.

> "While He was still a young man the tide of popular opinion turned against him. His friends ran away. One of them denied him, another betrayed him. He was turned over to his enemies. He went through the mockery of a trial. He was nailed to a cross between two thieves. His executioners gambled for the only property He had while on earth while he was dying, and that was his coat. When He was dead, He was laid in a borrowed grave through the pity of a friend.

> "Twenty-one centuries have come and gone, and today He is the central figure of the human race and the leader of the column of progress. I am far within the mark when I say that all the armies that ever marched, and all the navies

that were ever built, and all the parliaments that ever sat, and all the kings that ever reigned, put together, have not affected the life of man upon this earth as powerfully as has this one solitary life."

Praise God indeed for the example of Jesus, who lived life the way that it was really meant to be lived.

Life Goals for true success

1. Take care of your mind and body

Why should we take care of our minds and bodies? First of all, you cannot separate them, they impact and are interdependent on each other. When you're sick you cannot think straight, when you are confused, you feel sick and can't move forward in some areas. Right? Secondly, it says in 1 Corinthians 6:19-20, *"do you not know that your bodies are temples of the Holy Spirit, who is in you, whom you have received from God? You are not your own; you were bought at a price. Therefore, honor God with your bodies."*

Our bodies are a gift from God. We may not always be happy with what we see in the mirror, but that is God's wisdom and sovereignty in our lives.

And for our minds, we read in Phil 4:8 *"Finally, brothers and sisters, whatever is true, whatever is noble, whatever is right, whatever is pure, whatever is lovely, whatever is admirable – if anything is excellent or praiseworthy – think about such things."*

Do we have a choice as to what we will think about?

Of course we do…because God has given us the power of choice and the gift of free will.

And He also told us what we should think about. So let's take care of our minds and our bodies.

2. Make every day count.

What does the bible have to say about that?

Well in Psalm 90:12 it says *"teach us to number our days, that we may gain a heart of wisdom."*

It *doesn't* mean that we think and worry about the possibility of only having a short time to live. It basically says, let us be cognizant of the fact that our earthly life is not forever. And you and I need to be intentional about making the most of our time.

Some people ask me, why I decided to go into full time. My wife told me before, as a way to encourage me, was that I would be the president of a company one day.

People have asked me why I decided to go full time. I tell them that one of the reasons is this: If my life span on earth will be like the life span of my father's. I only have 11 years left on this earth. If my life span will be like my older brother, I only have 5 years left. So I needed to make a decision, what I would do with rest of my life.

Does that make sense?

Did the Word of God say that we need to learn how to number our days, so that we may gain a heart of anxiety…or regret?

No, it says, "Teach us to number our days so that we may gain a heart of wisdom."

And of course in Romans 12:1 we are told, *"Therefore, I urge you, brothers and sisters, in view of God's mercy, to offer your bodies as a living sacrifice, holy and pleasing to God – this is your true and proper worship."*

It means that every day that we wake up in bed and we can breathe, do stuff, and do things that God wants us to do as an act of worship, let's do these with thanksgiving, in awe and with gratitude to God.

3. Prioritize relationships

Prioritize relationships – first with God, and then with people.

In 1938 there was a study done by Harvard Institution called The Harvard Longitudinal Study of Adult Development – that was conducted on 724 young men. It's probably the longest study that was ever sustained by any organization, the study went on for 75 or more years.

What they did was they would visit these 724 men every year, to interview them and their family members, they would even take their blood samples, scan their brains, and perform a thorough examination.

Why?

Because they really wanted to know, what caused people to be healthy and happy? That was the objective of the study.

What was the single most outstanding factor that the study arrived at? What was the secret?

This was the conclusion: The happiest and healthiest among the group were those who had good quality relationships. Those were their findings.

And no wonder Jesus said this, when someone asked Him what is the greatest commandment.

What did Jesus say?

First, *"Love the Lord your God with all your heart and with all your soul and with all your mind. This is the first and greatest commandment. And the second is like it: "Love your neighbor as yourself."*

Remember our last point? Prioritize relationships – but first with God and then with people. And that is the same order as how Jesus stated it. Love the Lord your God and love others.

Perhaps you are here today, and you are trying to do so many other things. But you realize your relationship with God is a question mark, because when we look at all the people we've just talked about, their success all goes back to their personal relationships with God.

The Lord Jesus is the one who made the greatest difference in their lives.

And no wonder Jesus said in the Book of Revelation (3:20 NIV) *"Here I am! I Stand at the door and knock. If anyone hears my voice and opens the door, I will come in and eat with that person, and they with me."*

In this Scripture, Jesus was not talking about your typical hospitality. When two people "break bread", or share a meal – it implies that it is the beginning of a life-long relationship.

So my friend, if you are here today, and you're facing all kinds of challenges, some more, some less – I guarantee you that if your *relationship* with God is *not what it's supposed to be*, all the other things will *not* fall into place. Because our relationship with God is the cornerstone of life.

Jesus said *"I am the way, the truth and the life. No one comes to the Father except through Me."* (John 14:6 NKJV)

How have you been living your lives today? Have you been taking care of the mind and body that God has entrusted to you?

Have we been making every day count by living by His priorities and not just ours?

How are our relationships with the people who should mean the most to us? Is there anything that we need to fix?

Perhaps like Moses we need to humble ourselves and take the initiative to apologize and reconcile.

But most important of all, how is our relationship with God? Do we have one in the first place?

If you've never given your life to Jesus, remember what He says, *"Here I am! I stand at the door and knock."* If you open the door of your heart and invite Him in, He will come in, and you will begin to have a relationship with the One who died on that cross, to pay for your sins and mine.

So what is your decision?

I hope that you pray to Him something like this:

> *"Lord Jesus I thank You for your amazing love for me. I thank you for displaying and demonstrating this love by dying on the cross for my sins. This is an act of faith, and I place myself entirely in Your hands, my earthly life, my eternal destiny, my need for forgiveness, my need to change — which I cannot do on my own power.*
>
> *"I surrender everything about myself to you today. Lord, would You come into my life and make me the person You want me to be*
>
> *"And Lord I know that with You in my life, even when my earthly days will be finished, I know that the best is yet to come, because I will spend eternity with you. This is my prayer, in Jesus' Name. Amen and amen."*

Left to Right (taken in Sydney, Australia): Pastor Ricky, his wife Agnes, grandchildren Isabel and TonTon, their daughter-in-law Tin, and their son Miguel.

ENRIQUE GARCIA SARTHOU

Enrique "Ricky" Sarthou graduated Magna Cum Laude with a B.S. Business Economics degree from the University of the Philippines (Diliman, Quezon City).

He was Vice President and head of Marketing Services, overseeing marketing and advertising, training, sales facilities and sales administration for Philam Life.

He later became Vice President and Regional Sales Head for ManuLife Philippines, where he bagged consecutive awards for Region of the Year and was Appointed Manulife's Senior Agency Directors.

He was Senior Vice President and Marketing Head of Generali Pilipinas, before he accepted the position as Executive Pastor of Christ's Commission Fellowship at their Main headquarters.

He has been married to Agnes for over 35 years. They have two children, Miguel and Abigail, both grown and married, and three grandchildren – Eumir, Isabel and Antonio.

THERE'S HOPE IN THE BIG C

By Agnes "Aggie" Sarthou

"Behold, I have refined you, but not as silver; I have tried you in the furnace of affliction." (Isaiah 48:10)

Over 16 years ago, the furnace of affliction burned hotter than normal.

I had just completed my doctoral studies when the tragic news came: *I was diagnosed with Stage 4 cancer.*

Cancer is like a "death sentence."

Extremely few miraculously survive metastatic cancer. Oftentimes, cancer patients die before their time, due to depression, worry, anxiety, and fear.

These toxic emotions fan the flame in the furnace of affliction.

Thankfully, I didn't go through depression but I didn't understand then God's game plan for my life.

I couldn't visualize a "happy ending" with stage 4 cancer.

I remember asking God: *"Lord, why did you allow me to complete my doctorate and then give me a terminal disease?"*

Then the Lord reminded me that He *didn't* need my credentials. He desired character.

I could be a better doctor if I became a patient first. Admittedly, I had a short fuse. I had been very impatient.

The fiery furnace of affliction with the big C has taught me compassion for the sick and drew me so much closer to God in ways that nothing else could.

I remember God's encouragement: *"When I walk through the fire, I will not be burned. The flames will not consume me."* (Isaiah 43:2)

While the furnace of affliction can be unspeakably hot, what I gained was indescribable hope and joy. I profoundly experienced God's supernatural healing of both body and spirit!

There is Healing

Psalm 23:1 Though I walk through the valley of the shadow of death, I fear no evil for He was with me.

My stormiest chemo days were my best times with God.

I had amazing one-on-one talks with Him. And during extreme bouts with nausea and pain, God carried me through.

He gave me unexplainable rest and sleep at the height of pain and suffering from my chemo sessions. These were times of rest and healing. Indeed, His mercies are new every morning.

I had to take a very expensive drug to tame my very aggressive and invasive cancer.

My doctor explained, that just like people, cancer has a "personality". The nature of my cancer was extremely "bugnutin" (easily angered and provoked). She likened it to a Rottweiler.

She explained further that the drug would make my cancer cells behave "like a poodle". Again, I asked God why He allowed stage 4 cancer. How did I get such a vicious, aggressive cancer that immediately metastasized to my 7th and 11th rib?

Then He reminded me of the story of Lazarus.

When he heard this, Jesus said, *"This sickness will not end in death. No, it is for God's glory so that God's Son may be glorified through it."* – John 11:4

I vividly recall my oncologist telling me, *"Aggie, I am a good doctor. But I am only a doctor. I am not God. You are stage 4. Only God can heal you."*

Had I been diagnosed with a lower stage cancer, people might attribute my healing to medicine, or to my doctor or to my great attitude.

But when God heals a stage 4 cancer patient, only *He* gets the glory!

There is **O**pportunity

Jeremiah 33:3 says *"Call to me and I will answer you and tell you great and unsearchable things you do not know."*

Affliction provides us great opportunities to bless and be blessed.

One big blessing that cancer gives is the opportunity to talk about Jesus.

In practically all my training programs, my cancer story has been my platform to share the love of Jesus, and His supernatural intervention in my life.

As I share His story in my life, I am blessed in return and inspired to see the transformation.

Around this time, I founded and became the Ministry Head of **Life to the Max** – a ministry at our church community.

Volunteers of Life to the Max are given the opportunity to serve those afflicted with cancer, as well as other chronic degenerative diseases. These volunteers give of their time, energy and resources to be a blessing to group members and first time guests.

God lavishly poured His love through family and friends. And my husband was my staunchest prayer partner and support. I would see him daily, on bended knees, humbly asking God to heal me.

Thousands of people also prayed for me. In fact, when a dear brother in Christ heard of my terminal condition, he confidently told me, "Aggie, a million are praying for you!"

What a blessing to be loved and prayed for!

There is a Peace

Cancer has a way of damaging every part of the patient's body, including one's pocketbook.

The 18 weekly chemo sessions did not depress me, but thinking about paying my medical bills did.

My medication alone cost about PhP200,000 [= US$4,000] every 21-28 days!

My operation practically wiped out our medical insurance.

Consequently, my chemo treatments required digging into our very limited funds.

In desperation, I went on a one-day "wailing time" with God. I remember telling God, "Lord, I will not die of cancer, but I will by paying off the medical bills."

> Philippians 4:6-7
> *"Do not be anxious for anything, but in prayer and supplication, with thanksgiving, make your requests to God. And the peace of God that transcends all understanding will fill your heart and mind in Christ Jesus."*

God's timing is impeccable! That same day, my husband handed me an envelope. It had several checks and some cash! The first check I saw was sufficient to pay for half of my first chemo! Indeed, He answers prayers in mysterious ways!

Then I cried harder… I heard His gentle rebuke saying, *"Oh, you woman of little faith, didn't I tell you, I would take care of you?!"*

So I stopped counting and started believing that He would provide. After all, He made everything – He owns everything!

If there wasn't be enough funds for the next treatment, I did not need to worry. My God would take care of me.

He also reminded me that the medicines would not heal me… only He could!

I realized that I should not unnecessarily complicate my life. Instead, I should simplify it by doing the things that are possible, and let God do the impossible.

There is an Eternity

Psalm 90:10,12
"Seventy years are given to us! Some even live to eighty. But even the best years are filled with pain and trouble; soon they disappear, and we fly away. Teach us to realize the brevity of life, so that we may grow in wisdom."

Our physical body is temporal… Our soul is eternal.

The truth is, there are only two destinations after we breathe our last. We can live in the presence of God for eternity, or we can be thrown into the lake of fire and brimstone where there is weeping and gnashing of teeth.

Sin is so much like cancer. While cancer kills the body, sin kills the soul.

God's word equates sin with death.

"For the wages of sin is death…" Romans 6:23a).

God knew the gravity of our sin problem. And much like cancer, we are completely helpless to solve it.

… *"But the gift of God is eternal life in Christ Jesus our Lord."* (Romans 6:23 b)

I remember, Jing Egenias, a Life Maxer who inspired us with her surrendered life. She would attend Life to the Max events despite her weak condition.

One day I asked Jing how she was coping with her terminal condition. She said, *"You know Tita Aggie, I don't have to be healed to praise God or be joyful. I know in the end, my God will heal me forever. HE will bring me to a place where there will be no more tears, no more sickness, where there is no more pain."*

Jing's life was a great reminder to keep an eternal perspective. She continued to say, *"For as long as God gives me life, and allows me to walk, I will choose to serve Him. I have to praise God because being alive today is already a miracle. As long as God breathes life into me, I will be grateful. I will not compare myself with others who are well. I can be content with what God gives me."*

John 3:16
"For God so loved the world that He gave His only Son, that whoever believes in Him shall not perish but have eternal life"

H = Healing
O = Opportunity
P = Peace
E = Eternity

The gift of HOPE is free… only because Jesus paid for it in full.

Wouldn't you be deeply grateful if someone paid for *all* your medical bills for a cancer-free life? This is exactly what Jesus did on the cross for you and me so that we could all be "spiritually cancer-free."

Ephesians 2:8-9
"For it is by grace you have been saved through faith – and this is not from yourselves, it is the gift of God – not by works, so that no one can boast."

Indeed, the gift of eternal life is free in Christ Jesus. We need not pay for the cure of our spiritual cancer. Our Lord Jesus Christ paid for it in full at the cross. Before He breathed His last, He cried out *"Tetelestai!"*, meaning PAID IN FULL.

God desires for us to spend eternity with Him in heaven. He finds no pleasure in seeing anyone eternally separated from Him.

And so He gives this invitation: *"Behold, I stand at the door and knock. If anyone hears my voice and opens the door, I will come in to him and eat with him, and he with Me."* Revelation 3:20 ESV

You can open the door of your life and accept the free gift of eternal life through a simple prayer such as this one…

> Lord Jesus, My Healer. I know that You hear me and You know my great affliction. I put my hope and trust in You alone for my physical and spiritual healing. I confess that I have sinned against You. Thank You for paying the debt of sin in full by your death on the cross.
>
> I accept the gift, Your gift of eternal life. Please come into my life – be my Savior and Master. Grant me to experience You even in the midst of my affliction. Make me the kind of person You want me to be. Amen.

If you sincerely prayed this prayer, we have Christ's assurance that He will never leave you nor forsake you. (Hebrews 13:5).

Yes, our only Hope is in the **Big C** … **Christ** in you. In Him, we have passed from death to eternal life.

Left to Right (taken in Sydney, Australia): Agnes's husband Pastor Ricky, Agnes, grandchildren Isabel and TonTon, their daughter-in-law Tin, and their son Miguel.

AGNES "AGGIE" C. SARTHOU, Ph.D.

Agnes "Aggie" Sarthou graduated with Honors earning a B.S. degree in Business Economics from the School of Economics at the University of the Philippines – Diliman, Quezon City.

She has an M.A. in Development Economics from Williams College in Williamstown, Massachusetts, and a Doctorate degree in Organization Development & Planning from the Southeast Asia Interdisciplinary Development Institute (SAIDI).

She was an Economist-Technical Staff for the Ministry of Finance, the Supervising Officer for the Office of the Prime Minister, and Manager of Internal Communications & Policy for the Bank of the Philippine Islands.

Later she became a Training Consultant for various Training Organizations including Salt and Light, Business, Works and Quintegral/ AMA. She was also Resident Trainer and Management Consultant for Wilcon Depot.

Aggie was the Founder and Ministry Head of Christ's Commission Fellowship's (CCF) Life to the Max Ministry.

She is married to Enrique Sarthou, who has been CCF's Executive Pastor for over 35 years. They have two children – Miguel and Abigail, both grown and married, and three grandchildren – Eumir, Isabel and Antonio.

CHAPTER 9

REFLECTIONS ON DIVINELY DESIGNED FAITH, HOPE AND LOVE

By Rev. Dante Eleazar "Bong" Simon

These are some of the meditations that come from from 45 years as a Christian believer in Jesus Christ, and 37 years as a servant of the Lord.

As the verses and words that have sustained me as a new Christian and a Christian minister.

My hope is that as they have sustained me and gave me hope, May the meditations of my mouth and the reflections of my heart be pleasing to God and edifying to the Body of Christ.

THE GOD OF CREATION O GOD HOW EXCELLENT ARE THE WORK OF YOUR HANDS!

St. Thomas Aquinas (1225-1274) fully understood the Trinitarian theology of creation. Each divine Person of the Godhead has a distinct mode of existence.

The Father eternally exists as the Source without origin, Who is the principle of the Word, with whom the Father breathes forth the Holy Spirit. The Father acts in the world through the Son who is the Word and Wisdom, and creates and gives life through the Holy Spirit who is Love in person.

Let us summarize Aquinas's thoughts: It is God's nature to exist. God is present in all His creation.

Creatures possess existence by participation.

Each expresses something of the divine likeness.

Each creature, each star in our galaxy, each sea creature is an expression of the Divine Artist who is God.

Each is a product of the Divine will and Divine Love. Each creature express the divine goodness.

The psalmist David said:

    A. Lord how majestic is Thy creation
    B. When I look at the heavens and the stars I see Your work
    C. What is man and woman that You are mindful of us?

The created work expresses and manifests a God of order and system. It is so ordered that there is a system and arrangement where every creature is where it should belong.

Listen to John Calvin's words:

1. Creation is revelatory of God' s existence.
2. Creation is the theatre of God's glory.
3. Creation is the mirror of God's nature and wisdom.
4. There must be amazement as we enjoy and delight in the glory, and the beautiful garment of God's work.
5. Therefore, since these are God's gifts, we are custodians and stewards of creation. We must preserve and enhance, not destroy what God requires us to preserve.

Reflection

1. Collaborative Author of "Unstoppable" Chen Mencias shares her delight and awe when she first dove into the sea. How about you? What emotions come to you when you experience the beauty and majesty in creation?
2. What must a Christian do in the light of environmental challenges?
3. There are some believers who came to know the Lord through observing creation. One such person was the subject of my brother Dodjie Simon's song "Sino Ka Man" which is a Filipino praise song describing such the awe-inspiring experience of a person who was deeply touched by creation. How did you come to know the Lord? Give thanks.

Prayer

Lord God, thank you for giving us this wonderful planet. Help us to be aware, to take care of it, and to pass it on the next generation. Amen.

GOD'S COMPASSIONATE LOVE

Psalm 116 *"Gracious is the Lord, and righteous is our God…yes our God is compassionate."*

John 3:16 *"For God so loved the world that He gave His one and only Son that whosoever believes in Him should not perish but have eternal life."*

Frederick Buechner describes what it means to have *compassion*.

Compassion is the capacity for feeling what it is like to live in somebody else's skin. It is the knowledge that there can never be peace or joy if the Lord doesn't give it to us.

The God of the Bible is One who feels for His people.

In the Old Testament God said (paraphrase): *I have seen the affliction of My people, I have heard their cry, I will save them.*

These characteristics of God show us a God who feels for us, and knows exactly what we are going through.

In the New Testament we find the Son of God Jesus Christ feels deeply for us. When He learned that His best friend Lazarus died, He wept.

When He saw the people on a hill, He was grieved because they were like sheep without a shepherd.

In the Holy Spirit, we have a Friend, a Defender, Teacher, Encourager, and One who stands side by side with us.

Indeed, the Triune God exemplifies a God who knows our travails, our challenges, our problems, our human situation.

Jesus was always moved by compassion. He was the epitome of love, compassion and concern for the other.

When He told a parable to explain who was our neighbor, he elevated a Samaritan in a good light, rather than a Pharisee or a priest!

One day, He walked by the roadside and two blindmen shouted: Jesus, have mercy upon us! Jesus stopped and looked at them and asked: "What do you want me to do for you?"

Jesus had *compassion*, touched their eyes and they were miraculously healed!

Jesus' compassion prompted Him to act, and even now, He mercifully loves, heals and forgives.

His very presence in the world show His compassion, God in the flesh One who is incarnate God, the God who walked with us and lived in our neighborhood. (based on John 1:14, The Message, Eugene Peterson).

Reflection

God's amazing love is beyond compare. *"For God so loved the world that He gave His only begotten Son that whosoever believes in Him should not perish but have everlasting love."* John 3:16 KJV

Prayer

Lord Jesus, thank You that You know what's going on in my life. Thank You that You know *exactly* all my needs, and You are able to hear me, feel my anguish, hear my cry, and deliver me from my misery.

Thank You because You are a compassionate God. *"Bless the Lord O My soul, and all that is within me, Bless His holy Name."* Psalm 103:1 KJV

I bless Your Name. Amen.

HOPE AGAINST HOPE

My Hope is In the Lord who made Heaven and Earth…

Romans 4:18 *"Who against hope believed in hope that he might be made the Father of many nations…"*

The phrase can be a perplexing and confusing one. Isn't *hope* a good thing?

Why would one need to *hope* against *hope*?

Well, the writer St. Paul was contrasting hope by itself vs. hope *anchored in faith*.

One commentary says the first kind of hope as mere probability.

The second kind of hope is an assured confidence, grounded on divine promise. The difference is that one hope is *based on human nature* and the other one on *divine promises*.

When one's hope is based on human promises, there is no certainty.

Thus, the saying: "Don't put your hopes up."

However when our hope is built on God's Word, it will surely come to pass because God's Word is true, accurate, and sure.

A hymnwriter wrote:

> *"My hope is built on nothing less than Jesus' blood and righteousness.*
> *I dare not trust the sweetest frame, but wholly lean on Jesus' name.*
> *On Christ the solid rock I stand*
> *All other ground is sinking sand*
> *All other ground is sinking sand."*

Reflection Questions

Edward Mote, the Lyricist of the above hymn wrote: *"On Christ the solid rock I stand, all other ground is sinking sand."*

What is your hope?

What is in your heart of hearts?

Who do you trust will deliver all His promises?

People will fail and disappoint , but God will always be faithful.

Prayer

Open my eyes that I may see, glimpses of Your truth and love. Forgive me, Lord when I have trusted in other gods and human promises. Teach me to only trust in You. Amen.

FUTURE GLORY

Romans 8:18-25 *"For I consider that the sufferings of this present time are not worth comparing with the glory that is to be revealed to us. 19 For the creation waits with eager longing for the revealing of the sons of God. 20 For the creation was subjected to futility, not willingly, but because of him who subjected it, in hope 21 that the creation itself will be set free from its bondage to corruption and obtain the freedom of the glory of the children of God. 22 For we know that s the whole creation t has been groaning together in the pains of childbirth until now. 23 And not only the creation, but we ourselves, who have the firstfruits of the Spirit, groan inwardly as we wait eagerly for adoption as sons, the redemption of our bodies. 24 For in this hope we were saved. Now hope that is seen is not hope. For who hopes for what he sees? 25 But if we hope for what we do not see, we a wait for it with patience."*

Pastor John Piper says: "The future glory of God prepared for us is not yet totally revealed to us, but includes the revealing of all that God has promised us."

The JB Philips translation states:

"The whole creation is on tiptoe as it awaits God's revelation and seeing the wonderful sight of God's children coming into their own... The future glory

includes the full renewal of creation, to its original design and purpose. The future glory includes our freedom from sin and its corruption, including the full redemption of our bodies."

Reflection

How do we look at pain, illness and natural disasters – knowing that the challenges we experience cannot compare to the glory that is to come?

How do we understand the future promise of glory for believers?

How does this develop into an attitude of hope?

Prayer

Lord, I thank You that You dwell in me and You abide in the worship of Your people. Help me to know You in all Your splendor. I want to worship You and see You in all of Your glory. Amen.

WORRY IS MY ENEMY

Jesus said: "Don't worry about what you shall eat or wear. Even the heathens worry about these things. The birds of the air don't toil but their heavenly Father takes care of them. But seek first the kingdom of God and all these things will be added to you."

The concordance of the Bible states that the word "worry" or "fear" is repeated 365 times in Scripture. It seems God has given us one tablet a day knowing that even well-meaning and mature believers fall into the trap of worrying.

My good friend Prof. Meyen Arcellana Hertzsprung mentions in the Collaborative Book "Unstoppable" that worry was her particular struggle. Worry grew larger when she got married. She worried about money, she worried about her children.

She continues: "The truth is we really don't have a lot of control over much things in life. Once in a while, we get caught by this realization: someone is diagnosed with cancer, or dies in their sleep, or gets into a car accident.

> *"We realize how much we take things for granted, and how much of life is God's grace. It is God's grace not education, not financial planning, not a career that has kept us going. I look back and say: God has faithfully provided more than enough."* ~Dr. Meyen Hertzsprung

John Wesley said: The best of all is that God is with us.

Reflection

Recall the times when you worried. What was it about?

How did you manage your worry?

Did you pray?

Was God faithful?

Jesus's Formula:

1. Don't worry.
2. Seek first God's kingdom.
3. Seek God's righteousness.
4. All these other things will be added to you. Note He did not say *some* things, but He said "*All* things will be added to you."

Prayer

Dear Lord, thank You for Your promise. Help me to fully trust in You and Your Word. Amen.

<hr/>

GIVE THANKS WITH A GRATEFUL HEART

Philippians 4:6 *"Do not be anxious about anything, but in everything by prayer and supplication with thanksgiving let your requests be made known to God."*

Psalm 30:12 *"That my glory may sing your praise and not be silent. O Lord my God, I will give thanks to you forever!"*

Isaiah 12:4-5 *"And you will say in that day: 'Give thanks to the Lord, call upon his name, make known his deeds among the peoples, proclaim that his name is exalted. Sing praises to the Lord, for he has done gloriously; let this be made known in all the earth.'"*

Hebrews 12:28-29 *"Therefore, since we receive a kingdom which cannot be shaken, let us show gratitude, by which we may offer to God an acceptable service with reverence and awe; for our God is a consuming fire."*

Jonah 2:9 *"But I will sacrifice to You With the voice of thanksgiving. That which I have vowed I will pay Salvation is from the Lord."*

1 Timothy 4:4-5 *"For everything created by God is good, and nothing is to be rejected, if it is received with gratitude; for it is sanctified by means of the word of God and prayer."*

Why should a Christian be thankful?

1. It helps us to be reminded of the Giver. Every good and perfect gift comes from God. (see James 1:17)
2. It makes us humble.
3. It reminds us to be good stewards.
4. It reminds us to share with others.
5. It give us the right perspective.

Someone once said: *"God lives in 2 places: In heaven and in a thankful and grateful heart."*

Reflection

A Checklist of things we can be thankful for…

Good health

- Money in the bank
- Job
- Good friends
- Freedom
- Parents
- Weekends
- Pets
- Learning from mistakes
- Health
- Healing
- Children
- Education
- Having a home
- Safety and security
- Time
- Clean water
- Love
- Books
- Kindness of strangers
- Rain and Trees
- Art
- Holidays
- Rainbows
- Tears
- Waking up to a new day

What shall I render to the Lord for all His benefits to me?

1. I could give praise to God. Psalm 34:3 says, *"O magnify the Lord. Let us exalt His name together."* This means lifting God's name up high, proclaiming utmost respect and praise to Him for all His benefits to us.
2. I could lift up His name in the gathering of His people. In the context of worship – praise and worship is integral in entering the holiness of God.
3. I could lift up the cup of salvation and call on the Name of the Lord.

The Matthew Henry's commentary states: *"To lift up the cup of salvation is symbolic of thanksgiving as in a feast."*

A good example is Holy Communion. "Call upon the name of the Lord" means to publish or preach the gracious nature of the Lord, and the great things He has done for us.

I could make offerings to the temple. We offer to God the sacrifice of praise, the firstfruits, and loving Him with all our soul, mind, heart and strength.

Prayers

Dear Lord, I thank you for the gift of life. Thank you for bringing the gift of wonderful people I have met along the journey. Some of them inspire me, stretch me, challenge me, love me and encourage me. All of them have helped me realize my potential. Thank you Lord. Amen.

A Parent's Prayer

Thank You for my children, Lord, I know they are a gift. Daily I need Your strength. Give me patience and love. Teach me the ways of Your love so I can share it with them.

Thanksgiving Prayer

Dear Lord, when I have food, help me remember the hungry.
When I have a home, help me to remember the homeless.
When I have job, remind me of those who have no jobs.
When I have no suffering, remind me of those who are suffering.
And when I have another coat or another pair of shoes, remind me
that they belong to the poor. Amen.

EVERY GOOD AND PERFECT GIFT COMES FROM GOD

The gifts of the Holy Spirit
The gift of Wisdom
The gift of knowledge
The gift of Faith
The gift of Healing
The gift of Miracles
The gift of prophecy
The gift of tongues
The gift of interpreting tongues
The gift of Administration
The gift of Helps

Jesus tells of a parable of three servants who were given and entrusted
with gifts or "talents."

In the other Gospels they were given money to invest.

My paraphrase:

There was a boss who was about to leave on a long journey. Before he did, he entrusted different gifts to his servants. He was gone for a long time, and when he came back, he wanted an accounting of how each servant had used the gifts.

So upon the master's return, the servants reported what they had done.

The first and second servants had worked so hard and reaped double the initial investment, for their efforts. The master said to each one: "Well done, good and faithful servant, enter into the joy of your Master."

The third one, unfortunately, did not do the same. He hid his talents by burying them in a hole in the ground, and did nothing to make the money grow.

The master was upset and mad. He took everything from the servant.

My good friend Winnie Arrieta who was one of my Collaborative Authors of the book "Unstoppable" mentions in her Chapter, that she was clear that the Lord wanted her to use her talents to glorify Yahweh.

At a young age, she left everything in Manila, Philippines to go and study abroad. It would be a life-changing journey but she was clear that that was what God wanted her to do. She lived and studied under the great maestros in Russia.

To date, Rowena Arrieta holds the distinction of being the only Filipina to study music and piano in the Soviet Union.

Questions for Reflections

1. How about you? What are the gifts and talents that God has given you?
2. What are you doing to hone and enrich those gifts?
3. How are you using it? To the best of your ability?

Prayer

Dear God, I thank you that You are a creative God. Thank You that You have given me gifts and talents so that I can use these to glorify Your Name and serve my neighbor.

Teach me to be humble. Teach me always to trust in You, knowing that "He who began a good work" in me is able to complete it. Teach me the way of righteousness.

Teach me how to cultivate and hone the gifts I have discovered…

the gifts I am discovering today….

and the gifts I will discover in the future…Amen.

GOD IS GOOD ALL THE TIME

Psalm 37:25 *"I have been young and now am old; yet I have not seen the righteous forsaken nor his seed begging for bread."*

This is a promise of God to all His children.

My mentor and friend, Rev. David Rodriguez always quoted this scripture as I was being trained under his wings as a novice pastor. He lived out this verse everyday as I watch him and learned the ropes of ministry at a young age of 19.

We usually hear this proclaimed at worship services: "God is good." And the people respond with: "All the time."

It takes a lot of faith and courage for people.

One of my Co-authors and schoolmate Atty. Beth Bacungan Macaibay (Collaborative Author, Unstoppable) wrote that her lifetime beliefs are: "Seize the day, laugh and laugh more."

I also like what she said: "Work hard and work well (I still have to learn this), share and enjoy your blessings, stay positive and believe in Him."

Her prayer-declaration is: *"God is good all the time."*

In my life of 58 years, I have been tested and tried over and over again…and every time God comes and delivers me from trouble, from illness and even from the pit.

I have walked through dark valleys and the valley of death and was fearful, but God gave me strength.

Many times I declare: *"God is faithful and His steadfast love endures forever."* And like Job, I say: *"The Lord gave, and the Lord has taken away; Blessed be the Name of the Lord."*

Somehow in the majestic wisdom of God, we come out victorious, we show faith, and God demonstrates His faithfulness.

I work as a hospice chaplain, I see illness and death everyday.

As of this writing my wife has recently endured a heart attack and a diabetic coma, and my eldest son is suffering from a long-time illness.

In the end I declare: *"God is Good all the time!"*

Reflection

When was the last time your faith was tested?

How did you handle the situation?

Looking back, what did you learn?

Did you experience God's faithfulness?

Prayer

Thank You, God for Great is Your faithfulness, O God my Savior. Though the mountains shake and the seas roar, You are faithful. Thank You that You are the same yesterday, today and forevermore. Praise Your Name, O God.

Experiencing a Living Faith

Read Joshua 2:8-14

Fierce Inner Struggles

The book of Psalms reveals the inner thoughts of those seeking God in a hostile world. We are allowed to witness firsthand the battles raging in their minds. We see their inner struggles.

We see those struggling to allow their faith in God to become an authentic guide to sustain them in their daily battles.

The Psalms reveal the intensity of the inner struggles of believers.

Read Psalms 5:1-12

Psalms 5 is a morning psalm of David.

The Psalm gives us a front row seat into the thoughts of David's heart as he faces his enemies.

David brings his faith to bear on his life. He awakens in the morning with an *intense* realization of the daily battles he faces. His enemies surround him.

Every battle begins and ends in our hearts.

Perhaps this could be what he was thinking: *"It doesn't matter, if I am herding sheep, fighting a lion, or ruling as a king, the battle is God's."*

We make the battles God's when we enter into the battle to give God the glory.

From start to finish David's battle was a spiritual battle between the earthly forces of evil pitted against the God of the universe. Yet, the real battlefield is centered in David's heart as he fully *trusts* in the Lord.

Years later as this same grown-up shepherd boy writes Psalm 5, we find him still relying upon God's deliverance. David's enemies are out to destroy him. And even all these years later, David is totally trusting God to stand against his enemies.

> *5 The arrogant cannot stand in your presence; you hate all who do wrong. 6 You destroy those who tell lies; bloodthirsty and deceitful men the LORD abhors.*

These words are written as David wrestles with his personal struggle with the intense evil seeking to engulf him. They are not words from a sanctimonious attitude of self-righteousness.

And David is always mindful of his personal *failings*. As you read through David's psalms you get to understand how well aware he was of his personal *failings*.

Read Psalms 6:1-5

The basis of coming to God is God's unfailing love — His mercy.

We might think we are *not righteous enough* to come to God with our request.

Well, no one is.

David recognizes that God takes no pleasure in evil. He knows he can only enter into God's presence through God's mercy. He is acutely aware of his personal failings.

The Israelites were suffering persecution in Isaiah's time. Evil was raging all around and it seemed as though God had hidden His face from them.

They were going into Babylonian captivity for their sins against God. They were suffering from God's judgment on Israel. They were in a place where they could see no evidence of God's presence.

Yet, the remnant of the faithful was determined to *live in expectation*.

Read Isaiah 8:17

During our personal struggles we may feel that God has hidden his face from us. Yet we must believe God is moving in our world to refocus our lives on what is truly important.

John's revelation sought to prepare Christians for the Roman persecution of Christians with these words.

> Revelation 13:9-10 NIV
> *9 He who has an ear, let him hear.*
> *10 If anyone is to go into captivity,*
> *into captivity he will go.*
> *If anyone is to be killed with the sword,*
> *with the sword he will be killed.*
> *This calls for patient endurance and faithfulness on the part of the saints.*

Daniel spent most of his life in Babylonian captivity.

It was a period when God actually hid his face from Israel.

It was during this period Daniel writes, *"Give ear, our God, and hear; open your eyes and see the desolation of the city that bears your Name. We do not make requests of you because we are righteous, but because of your great mercy. O Lord, listen! O Lord, forgive! O Lord, hear and act! For your sake, O my God, do not delay . . . "* Daniel 9:17-19 NIV

Daniel recognizes the only way for him to approach God is through His mercy. It is the only way to discover salvation. That is exactly what Daniel does throughout his life. Oh how God's glory is revealed through Daniel's life.

I think Daniel knew something about David's struggles.

David writes in Psalm 5:7-8 NIV – *But I, by your great love, can come into your house; in reverence I bow down toward your holy temple. 8 Lead me, Lord, in your righteousness because of my enemies — make your way straight before me.*

The Bible makes it abundantly clear that God's mercy is readily available.

Matthew 7:7-12 NIV

7 "Ask and it will be given to you; seek and you will find; knock and the door will be opened to you. 8 For everyone who asks receives; he who seeks finds; and to him who knocks, the door will be opened. 9 Which of you, if his son asks for bread, will give him a stone? 10 Or if he asks for a fish, will give him a snake? 11 If you, then, though you are evil, know how to give good gifts to your children, how much more will your Father in heaven give good gifts to those who ask him! 12 So in everything, do to others what you would have them do to you, for this sums up the Law and the Prophets."

Troubles are troubles regardless of their character.

Do you think the biblical stories are too ancient to be relevant?

The precepts revealed through each story – have modern day application. The precepts only come alive for us through meditating on God through Scripture.

Each day brings its own diverse problems for each of us.

Jesus said, "…each day has enough troubles of its own" (Matthew 6:34).

Job says man born of woman is full of troubles.

We might think the saints who jotted down their thoughts or who penned the Scriptures were immune to problems.

This was *never* the case.

They were usually writing about their problems as they struggled to believe — they struggled to live righteously.

It is the theme of every biblical story.

The psalmist sees the big picture. He knows the potential of evil raging from without and within. He reminds himself that God is in control. He lays out his desire with eager expectation.

His prayer is centered in the mercy of God. He prays "Lead me, O LORD, in your righteousness because of my enemies—make straight your way before me."

He doesn't come to God with a well laid out plan to defeat his enemies. He simply asks God to lay out his righteous path before him.

He desires to clearly see the path God makes for him. He takes his thoughts captive as he focuses on obedience to God.

> 2 Corinthians 10:3-6 NIV
> *3 For though we live in the world, we do not wage war as the world does. 4 The weapons we fight with are not the weapons of the world. On the contrary, they have divine power to demolish strongholds. 5 We demolish arguments and every pretension that sets itself up against the knowledge of God, and we take captive every thought to make it obedient to Christ.*

Our Lives Become the Basis of Worship

Our spiritual battles become the very context out of which our worship flows.

Throughout the Bible we see the lives of the faithful become the very subject and motivation for worship. *Their battles* became their avenue of reliance upon God.

Two of the main themes of the psalms are: i) the struggles of the psalmist and ii) they end with worship.

The psalms were written as private meditations about the spiritual battles the writers faced. The psalms were journals of their private hymns of praise. They were sung by the choir. They were read as prayers. They were reminders of who God had been to them, who He is, and how he sustains them.

God is worshipped as their lives become the subject of worship—the content from which worship flows. Their lives become the content of praise to God.

David's troubles and his reliance upon God is the theme of his psalms.

He rises in the morning expectantly laying his life out before God. His head is not buried in the sand. He is intent on focusing his life on God—intent on making God his refuge.

These struggles become the subject of worship as the psalms are written for his personal worship and are read or sung in corporate worship.

God is certainly the object of their worship, but the *content* of their lives became the heart and soul of worship.

Today we attend church expecting the church, to make it all exciting.

David had his private meditations about the battles he faced read aloud in the assembly. His life created the excitement for worship as he shared his thoughts and struggles with the assembly. His God-given victories made worship real, exciting and personal.

We see this in the Corinthian letter.

2 Corinthians 1:8-11 NIV

8 We do not want you to be uninformed, brothers, about the hardships we suffered in the province of Asia. We were under great pressure, far beyond our ability to endure, so that we despaired even of life. 9 Indeed, in our hearts we felt the sentence of death. But this happened that we might not rely on ourselves but on God, who raises the dead. 10 He has delivered us from such a deadly peril, and he will deliver us. On him we have set our hope that he will continue to deliver us, 11 as you help us by your prayers. Then many will give thanks on our behalf for the gracious favor granted us in answer to the prayers of many.

The life experiences of first century Christians were the driving force of their worship and fellowship.

Paul's problems forced him to rely on the God who raises the dead. It was there he found deliverance. His deliverance becomes the motivation for the Corinthians' worship as they read what he pens to the assembly.

The problems of the first Christians drove them *not only* to rely on God, but on each other as they helped one another through prayer. As they helped one another through prayer, they were inspired to give thanks to God for His gracious favor granted, in answer to those prayers.

Worship must be seen as a way of life to be embraced among believers that overflows into the assembly of the saints.

I am perplexed when I read First Corinthians. The church in Corinth was overwhelmed with problems. And when I read Second Corinthians, it reveals that they were well on their way to solving their problems…praise God!

I am confused when the same Corinthian letters do not have the same effect on the problems of modern day Christians.

What is the problem?

Is it that we study the Bible for mere knowledge? Is it that we preach it to impart knowledge?

We try to understand the subjects of speaking in tongues—spiritual gifts—gender roles to abide by, in and out of the church. We debate the resurrection.

Simply discussing these subjects is enough to divide most churches. Yet, it was the very discussion of these subjects that brought unity to the Corinthian believers.

It could be your life. Just remember. Your personal battles *can* become God's battles. It is your choice.

When you allow that to happen, God is glorified and victory is assured.

Reflection

How do we survive in an evil world?

What do we do when surrounded by overwhelming forces of evil?

How do we respond when pursued by evil?

How do we handle our internal struggles?

How do we travel through the devil's maze without getting lost?

Prayer

Come Lord Jesus, Come!

LIFE IN THE SPIRIT

Romans 8:1-6 NIV *"There is therefore now no condemnation for those who are in Christ Jesus. 2 For the law of the Spirit of life has set you free in Christ Jesus from the law of sin and death. 3 For God has done what the law, weakened by the flesh, l could not do. By sending his own Son in the likeness of sinful flesh and for sin, he condemned sin in the flesh, 4 in order that the righteous requirement of the law might be fulfilled in us, who walk not according to the flesh but according to the Spirit. 5 For those who live according to the flesh set their minds on the things of the flesh, but those who live according to the Spirit set their minds on the things of the Spirit. 6 For to set the mind on the flesh is death, but to set the mind on the Spirit is life and peace."*

In philosophy or religion the professor asks: Are we bodies with spirit or spirit beings with flesh? Or are we both?

St. Paul in Romans 8 reminds us that though we are in the flesh, God has given us His Holy Spirit and if the Spirit lives in us, several things happen…

1. We are no longer condemned.
2. We are free from the bondage of sin and the law.
3. We are given the mind of the Spirit of Christ.
4. We are dead to sin, but alive in Christ.

We can understand the mind of Christ and therefore follow and become spiritually alive in Christ.

Reflection

How and why would St. Paul say (paraphrase): "that which I should not do I do and the things I should I don't?"

What are hindrances to a spirit-filled life?

How can we experience the fulness of the fruit of the Spirit?

Prayer

Lord Jesus, thank you that You who began a good work in me will complete it. Make me, mold me, use me to be a fruitful Christian everyday. Amen.

<hr />

HOLY SPIRIT, MY FRIEND

Romans 8:28 NASB *"And we know that God causes all things to work together for good to those who love God, to those who are called according to His purpose."*

This statement is the title of the book of Dr. David Cho, Pastor of Yoido Full Gospel church in Korea with over a million church members, known for their prayer services and prayer mountains. In this groundbreaking book he shares his secret of growing his small church from a few hundred people to over a million believers.

He says the secret is making the Holy Spirit his friend, the Persona of the Father and the Son.

The Holy Ghost later more popularly known as the Holy Spirit, is said to be the least known Person of the Trinitarian God. While we know God the Father and the Son, very few know that the Holy Spirit shares the same power, God-nature and persona of the Trinity.

Of course the Pentecostals have long discovered this truth in their use of the full spectrum of the Holy Spirit's giftings.

My good friend Isabel Dulce Mendoza Briones – at the end of her chapter in the book "Unstoppable" – shares of a time when she was needing directions.

She shares: *"I was unsure whether to leave my very first serious business for good. I had spent years doing it…but felt it was time to do something different."* She found herself at a contemplative Carmelite Sister's retreat house.

Reflection

Holy Spirit, thank You for being my friend. Thank You for being my light, my guide and my lamp to My path.

Prayer

Holy Spirit, guide me always. Lead Me in Your righteousness. Amen.

HEIRS WITH CHRIST

Read Romans 8:12-17

In Keep Believing Ministries, Dr. Pritchard reminds us of the three gifts of the Spirit to every believer.

1. The new believer receives a new mind

The only way we are transformed is by the transformation of the mind by diligent reading and studying the Word of God.

Spiritual metamorphoses happen with careful, deliberate, intentional study of God's Word. As you study the Word, the way you think slowly changes. And as a person thinks, so his or her life will change.

2. The believer receives a new nature

The true believer has the Holy Spirit indwelling in him or her. The Holy Spirit literally lives within you. Your body is dead to sin but alive to righteousness. The flesh cannot know the things of God. Only our spirits connect with the Spirit of God.

3. The Christian receives a new identity

    a.   We are no longer strangers but called children of God
    b.   We are given personal guidance by the Holy Spirit
    c.   We are heirs to God's riches
    d.   We can call God "Abba, Father!"

Reflection

How is it with your soul?

How are you growing in God's grace?

How much time do you spend in studying God's word?

How are you experiencing the transformation of the mind?

Prayer

O Lord, by the power of the Holy Spirit, this week, I will say yes to forgiving my enemies, loving everyone, not just the lovable, and going the second mile.

I also say yes to personal purity, a disciplined life, a gentle spirit, sharing Christ with friends, praying for others and the world, taking a step of faith, being faithful in giving my time, talents, treasure and service, trusting God even in the midst of fear and crisis, telling the truth, **and** experiencing the joy of the Lord.

A New Heaven and Earth

Read Revelation 21:1-2 (NIV)

> *"Then I saw "a new heaven and a new earth," [a] for the first heaven and the first earth had passed away, and there was no longer any sea. 2 I saw the Holy City, the new Jerusalem, coming down out of heaven from God, prepared as a bride beautifully dressed for her husband."*

The "second coming" is the term used to refer to the future event when the Lord Jesus will return to Earth, conquer His enemies, and reign as King of the world.

Jesus described His return in Matthew 24:30 – *"Then will appear in heaven the sign of the Son of Man, and then all the tribes of the earth will mourn, and they will see the Son of Man coming on the clouds of heaven with power and great glory."*

The Apostle John saw the Lord Jesus as a mighty warrior in Revelation 19:11-16 – *"Then I saw heaven opened, and behold, a white horse! The one sitting on it is called Faithful and True, and in righteousness he judges and makes war. His eyes are like a flame of fire, and on his head are many diadems, and he has a name written that no one knows but himself. He is clothed in a robe dipped in blood, and the name by which he is called is The Word of God. And the armies of heaven, arrayed in fine linen, white and pure, were following him on white horses. From his mouth comes a sharp sword with which to strike down the nations, and he will rule them with a rod of iron. He will tread the winepress of the fury of the wrath of God the Almighty. On his robe and on his thigh he has a name written, King of kings and Lord of lords."*

Implications

1. The Bible tells us that there was a beginning (Genesis), and there will be an end (The Revelation of Jesus Christ). This is a linear view of history. After the passing away of the first heaven and the first earth, there will be a new heaven and a new earth.

2. Christ as Savior dying on the cross will be replaced with *Christus Victor*, the victorious Christ who will come as Judge. He will no longer be the baby in the manger or the crucified Christ – but the victorious Son of God.

3. There will be a judgment day. Matthew talks about the separation of goats and sheep, people separated either to the left side or to right side. Christ will say to some, "I never knew you; depart from Me..."

4. How will the new heaven and earth look like? People have focused on a new heaven, how about the new earth?

Reflection

1. If Christ is coming back and soon, what does it mean for our lifestyle?
2. What does it mean for evangelism?
3. How should we look at the world events?
4. What about a theology of hope?
5. What priorities should we have?
6. What are your thoughts on this saying: *"Live simply so that others may simply live."*

Prayer

Come, Lord Jesus. Let Your kingdom come.

The Best of All is that God is with Us - John Wesley

Read Romans 8:31-32, 38-39 NIV

31 What then shall we say to these things? If God is for us, who can be against us? 32 He who did not spare his own Son but gave him up for us all, how will he not also with him graciously give us all things? 38 For I am sure that neither death nor life, nor angels nor rulers, nor things present nor things to come, nor powers, 39 nor height nor depth, nor anything else in all creation, will be able to separate us from the love of God in Christ Jesus our Lord.

Wikipedia contributors. "John Wesley." *Wikipedia, The Free Encyclopedia.* Wikipedia, The Free Encyclopedia, 11 Jun. 2020. Web. 20 Jun. 2020.

"John Wesley was an English cleric, theologian and evangelist who was a leader of a revival movement within the Church of England known as Methodism. The societies he founded became the dominant form of the independent Methodist movement that continues to this day.

"On 24 May 1738 he experienced what has come to be called his evangelical conversion, when he felt his "heart strangely warmed". He subsequently left the Moravians, beginning his own ministry.

"His evangelicalism, firmly grounded in sacramental theology, maintained that means of grace sometimes had a role in sanctifies of the believer, however he taught that it was by faith a believer was transformed into the likeness of Christ, and the good works are the evidence that a person has been so. He encouraged people to experience Jesus Christ personally in the 'more excellent way' of 'Christian perfection'."

"Wesley's teachings, collectively known as Wesleyan theology , continue to underpin the doctrine of the Methodist churches."

There are about 60 million Christians who trace their roots to the Wesley brothers.

Wesley believed in key principles:

1. That God is an all loving and saving God
2. We are saved by grace through faith.
3. That there are means of grace which include the sacraments, holy conferencing, Christian fellowship, prayer, worship and service.

Some of the thoughts of John Wesley include:

a. If we cannot think alike, can we at least love alike?
b. In minors, let us have liberty. In majors let us have unity. In all things let us have charity.
c. Do all the good you can, to all the people you can, in all the places you can, in all the ways you at all times.
d. Earn all you can, save all you can, give all you can.

The brothers John and Charles Wesley continued their ministry throughout

England and beyond.

The Rev. Charles Wesley wrote his theology in almost 3,000 hymns.

The Rev. John Wesley preached in all places in England and America and contributed to the great revival in England and Europe.

The brothers Revs. John and Charles Wesley believed in a God who is the Great shepherd, who provides for everything, who restores the soul. This God is all about saving grace, justifying grace, prevenient grace and sanctifying grace. The Methodist believers always believed in Open Doors, Open Hearts and Open Minds.

The Wesley brothers always preached and lived out God' s everlasting love and

grace.

On his deathbed , John was quoted: *"After everything in life, the best of all is that God is with us."*

Reflection Questions

1. Have you accepted Jesus as Lord and Savior of your life?
2. What is your rule in your life ? I s it to glorify God and serve Him forever?
3. When you leave planet earth, how will people remember you?
4. We always hear the saying: Only one life to live.

There is a song that states:

Only one life, only one will soon be past
Only what's done for Christ will last.

Ponder upon the above lyrics.

Prayer

Dear Lord, thank You so much for all Your love and grace. Thank You for offering Yourself as a sacrifice and dying for my sins. Thank You that You give me another chance in life. Thank you for blessing upon blessing. Thank you that I need not fear for You are with me. *"Your rod and staff they comfort me. Surely goodness and mercy shall follow me all the days of my life and that I shall dwell in the house of the Lord forever."*

Standing Left to Right: Dante Jr., David and Stephen.
Sitting: Pastor Eleazar "Bong" and his wife Vivelyn

REV. DANTE "BONG" SIMON

Rev. Dante "Bong" Simon is an Ordained United Methodist minister. Having been trained in the Philippines and the United States he has pastored churches from 50 to 500 members in the last 35 years.

Presently he is Spiritual Care Director of Promedica Heartland for Northern California.

He loves singing, drawing, writing poems, gardening and storytelling. Rev. Simon is blessed and happily married to Vivelyn Pascual and blessed with 3 wonderful sons David, Stephen and Dante Jr.

CHAPTER 10

LOOK INTENTLY

By Rolland Wright

H ave you ever spent a block of time *looking intently* into anything?

Those with graduate degrees have spent countless hours researching a specialty in their area of discipline, such as science, mathematics, medicine, or engineering. They have utilized technology to expand the depth into which they might explore a molecule, a cell or see into space. Our various interests compel us to travel to outer space, delve the depths of the oceans or attempt to conquer inner space. But have *you looked intently* into something, *anything*?

If you have loved, you most likely have looked into the eyes of your lover. If you have birthed a child, you probably have looked into the eyes of a miracle. If you have a pet, you have probably spent hours looking into their eyes. What did you see in them? What did the mirror of their eyes *reveal* to you?

We all look at ourselves in the mirror as we comb our hair and brush our teeth. As children, we all probably focus on some aspect of our appearance that we feel is embarrassing. We may feel extremely sensitive about something asymmetrical about our face. I recall thinking that my ears stuck out awkwardly from my head.

Then, overnight we morph into teenagers and begin to compare and scrutinize ourselves to a greater degree. The archaic, metal, full-band braces I endured throughout junior high school were **brutal! Painful**! As if body image or braces were not enough, acne exploded onto the scene. All of this can result in more time in front of a mirror, reflecting on all our imperfections.

Transparency

When I was approaching my sixties, I heard a recovery group leader share her family's story in front of a church body. I will never forget her transparency. She and her husband had served as missionaries. They later divorced and their two boys experienced a life of drugs and incarceration.

I had heard testimonies, before, many with which I could not identify. But her brokenness, humility and total transparency before God and everyone made a huge impact on me. I left that meeting, went home and wrote out my own story.

Truthfulness

The more I scrutinized my life, the more convicted I became. As I wrote, I realized that I had been living a life of self-deceit. I did *not* recognize the man I wrote about.

The Holy Spirit was convicting me through the Word and performing spiritual surgery as only He can. Hebrews 4:12 and 13 explains:

> *"For the word of God is living and active and sharper than any two-edged sword—piercing right through to a separation of soul and spirit, joints, and marrow, and able to judge the thoughts and intentions of the heart. No creature is hidden from Him, but all are naked and exposed to the eyes of Him to whom we must give an account.* (Tree of Life Version)

I felt naked and exposed to the truth about myself. I realized I had become self-deceived. I had compared myself with those around me. I felt that I was better than most and, thereby, I was ok. What a compromised life I was living! I knew I was settling for far less than what God had in store for me.

Today is the Day

Hebrews chapters 3 and 4 repeat the phrase, *"Today if you hear His voice, do not harden your hearts as in the rebellion."* (Heb. 3:7, 15, 4:7)

I became aware that I could not wait. I felt a sense of urgency. I knew what I had to do, and I did it! I repented to God for a season of involvement with pornography. I asked Him to forgive me for multiple marriages *and* divorces and the resulting collateral damage to my relationships—*especially* with my children and my parents.

I established a lifestyle of daily time in the Word of God. I rebuilt my relationship with God and asked my parents' forgiveness for the embarrassment I brought to the family. As of this writing, I am still seeking to repair and restore the relationships with my children.

Why do I share this?

I am pleading with you not to harden your heart. If you have been living in rebellion, apart from God, yield to Him today. Today is the appointed time to respond to His call. There is no other time, no better time. The urgency is "today"! Please do not wait!

Benefits

How does one yield to God? First, we are told to *"confess our sins to one another"* according to James 5:16. Why do we need to confess to one another? I believe there are several benefits:

The rest of the verse states: *"so that you may be healed."* Most of us *want* to be healed of many things, including illnesses. But one reason we are *not* healed is because we *will not* repent. While we may be more concerned about what others might think or how it might look, true repentance is *complete brokenness* and results in turning away from past behavior and following Jesus.

When I truly understood this verse, I desired to be healed! It did not matter to me what anyone else was thinking. I absolutely wanted to be freed from the tyranny of guilt I felt from my past.

I can certainly say that the decision to repent has resulted in the Holy Spirit continuing to transform, renew, restore, and repurpose me. People will have their opinions, but I *know* that I am not the same man.

Humility is another benefit of repentance. If you want to be like Jesus and be conformed to His image, you will need to humble yourself and repent to Him. There is no shortcut, and simply saying, *"I'm sorry"* does not cut it.

Perhaps the greatest benefit is submission. I made a commitment to God in my mid-twenties to live my life for Him by way of full-time ministry. I thought I had disqualified myself with multiple marriages and divorces. The institutional church did much to reinforce my feelings.

During the time I was repenting and being restored, a friend shared a scripture with me: *"For the gifts and calling of God are irrevocable"* (Romans 11:29). In other words, as much as I had messed up, God was saying, "You cannot undo what I have done." As a result, I am reconciled, redeemed, restored, reconditioned, reclaimed, and repurposed! I am His. Wonderfully His! Amazing grace! His mercies are new every day!

The book of James, authored by the half-brother of Jesus, has become one of my favorite books in the Bible. One of the shorter books, yet it is no less important.

So much of my life has been influenced by the first chapter where James exhorts us to *"rejoice in trials," "ask God for wisdom," and "endure testing"*. He *reminds us that "temptation does not come from God," but "every good gift comes from God"*. He exhorts us to *"Be doers of the word," "Be quick to listen, slow to speak, and slow to anger"*. He reminds us that *"Pure and undefiled religion before God and Father is this: to care for orphans and widows in their distress and keep oneself unstained by the world."*

Isn't the first chapter rich in instruction?

In addition, in James 1:23-25, the Tree of Life Version states:

> *For if anyone is a hearer of the word and not a doer, he is like a man who looks at his natural face in a mirror—for once he looks at himself and goes away, he immediately forgets what sort of person he **was**. But the one who **looks intently** into the **perfect Torah**, the Torah that gives freedom, and continues in it, not becoming a hearer who forgets but **a doer who acts—he shall be blessed in what he does**.*

Here we are told that the true mirror is Jesus. He is the Perfect Torah, the Perfect Law. We can compare ourselves to others and we will look pretty good, but when we compare ourselves to the Perfect One, we will not measure up.

Notice that when we look into a mirror, we are looking "past tense", *"he immediately forgets what sort of person **he was**."* Jesus tells us who we *are*…and who we *were*. We once *were* lost in sin.

For a complete overview, I invite you to read Romans 1:18-32 and 2 Timothy 3:1-7. It is not a pretty picture.

The whole list in 2 Timothy was convicting to me but I was most struck by was vs. 5, "holding to an outward form of godliness but denying its power. Avoid these people!" I felt like David when Nathan said to him, *"You are the man!"*

I was the exposed man that James was describing, and I was broken.

I share my story because I believe there are men who have been in the church all their lives and have fallen and been ensnared by temptation, trapped in a cycle that you cannot escape. You have lived a captive life for way too many years.

I want to implore you to *repent* and turn from your sin and look to Jesus! There is hope and restoration available at the foot of the Cross. *I am living proof.* What He has done in transforming my life, He can and will do for you.

And the benefits have been immeasurable!

A new life!

During my transformation, the Word came alive! Now, I look forward to coming into the presence of God every day.

My life verse is Acts 17:28 "In Him we (I) live and move and have our (my very) being." He is everything. Truly, He has restored me, reclaimed me, and repurposed me. He has given me new purposes for living for Him.

There was an academy award winning movie called *Chariots of Fire*, based on a true account of an Olympic athlete. His primary line in the movie was, ***"When I run, I feel God's pleasure."*** It is an awesome feeling to discover your life's "do"—your destiny, calling and purpose—and to feel God's pleasure while you are doing it!

How about you? Do you know your purpose?

What now?

If, because of hearing my story of repentance, reconciliation, and restoration, you have been motivated today to repent and turn your life around, I want to encourage you to do **three** things:

First, write out your story. Look intently into the "Perfect Torah" and pour it all out onto paper. Do not leave out any detail as this is a full "come-to-Jesus" meeting which leaves no hidden sin unrevealed. Revealing our hidden sin brings it out into the light and renders it entirely powerless.

Secondly, immediately email or hand-carry your story to your closest two or three Christian friends. (You may want to keep this between same-gender friends.) Please notice that I *did not* say publish your story or stand before your local church. It will be tough to be transparent before your friends, but how sincerely do you want to be healed? How desperately do you want to forsake your former life and walk in a new lifestyle with Jesus? Though you may experience accompanying feelings of humiliation, *if you do not do this step, you will find it easy to repeat past behaviors.*

Be sure to share only with friends who will not condemn you but will love you for the transparent action you have taken. This is vitally important, as your true friends will hold you accountable for the decision and repentance you have made and "declared."

You may even find that your friends will also want to write and share their story.

Thirdly, you will need to support your new life by developing a daily lifestyle of reading God's Word.

I suggest Wayne Cordeiro's book, *The Divine Mentor.* By implementing Cordeiro's principles, I have taught myself how to eat spiritual food. I have dined on the Word *daily* for about 15 years by using his system to make a practical application from the reading. As a result, the Holy Spirit has *transformed* my life *by* His Word.

You **must** get into the Word because it will become *life* to you and *alive* to you. This is a non-negotiable part of your new lifestyle in Jesus, *"for in Him we live and move and have our being"* (Acts 17:28, NKJV).

God wants to have preeminence, ***first place*** in everything, including your heart. If your desire is to claim or reclaim *your* Divine Design, or if you want to get into or get back into right relationship with Jesus, please do me the favor of writing to me at Rolland@firstplaceministries.com.

This article launches **First Place Ministries** based on Colossians 1:18b TLV *"...that He might come to have **first place** in all things."*

About **First Place Ministries**: We are a ministry of reconciliation. We seek to reconcile every man, woman, and child to God, then to each other. Our focus is with adults who have adult children that are disenfranchised from their birth family. We are a ministry focused on the Word of God, especially on the training of a daily Berean lifestyle. www.firstplaceministries.com

Left to Right: Rolland, Mike & Elaine (Rolland's sister), Ellen (Rolland's sister) & Glenn; Rolland's Mom & Dad - Marcella & Herman, Linea (Rolland's Dad's only sister), Rae (Rolland's Mom's sister) & Howard

ROLLAND WRIGHT

Rolland Wright is the founder and president of The Widows Project, a non-profit addressing the spiritual, emotional, and physical concerns of widows and widowers. www.thewidowsproject.org

He has a son Chris married to Cindy (2 daughters Chloe & Brenna); 2 daughters, Jennifer married to Nick (son Carter & daughter Kaylee) and Bethany (daughter Brooke).

His two (2) life verses are, Acts 17:28 "for in Him we live and move and have our being" (TLV) and Colossians 1:18b "that He might come to have first place in everything." (NASB). He holds a bachelor's degree from Biola University,

He enjoys writing and playing various board or card games. Social engagements are always on the calendar with friends.

PLEASE RATE OUR BOOK

My Collaborative-Authors and I would be honored if you would take a few moments to rate our book on Amazon.com (U.S.).

Or, if you're in any of these countries, please use these Amazon sites:

Amazon.ca (Canada)
Amazon.com.au (Australia)
Amazon.de (Germany)
Amazon.com.mx (Mexico)
Amazon.co.uk (U.K.)
Amazon.fr (France)
Amazon.co.jp (Japan)
Amazon.es (Spain)

A 5-star rating *and* a short review (e.g. "Incredible lessons!" or "Thoroughly enjoyed it!") would be much appreciated. We welcome longer, positive comments as well.

If you feel like this book should be rated at three stars or fewer, please hold off posting your comments on Amazon. Instead, please send your feedback directly to me (Jackie), so that we can use it to improve the next edition. We're committed to providing the best value to our customers and readers, and your thoughts can make that possible.

You can reach me at CustomerStrategyAcademy@gmail.com.

Thank you very much!

To your success and prosperity with a purpose,

Jackie Morey

Publisher-Collaborative Author
CustomerStrategyAcademy@gmail.com

www.ingramcontent.com/pod-product-compliance
Lightning Source LLC
LaVergne TN
LVHW011218080426
835509LV00005B/186

Where the Lion Roars

An 1890 African Colonial Cookery Book

By

A. R. B. (Mrs A. R. Barnes)

EDITED BY

David Saffery

JEPPESTOWN

Published by Jeppestown Press,
10A Scawfell St, London, E2 8NG, United Kingdom.

First published as *The Colonial Household Guide*, by Darter
Brothers and Walton, Cape Town, South Africa, 1890.

Introduction and commentaries © Copyright David Saffery 2006

Cover design © Copyright Chris Eason 2006

Front cover features *Cottages at Karoo National Park*, by Gemma
Longman, 2006; www.flickr.com/photos/g-hat/. Back cover shows
Kitchen, Stellenbosch Village Museum, Stellenbosch, South Africa, by Mike
Wong 2006; www.flickr.com/photos/squeakymarmot/.
Both reproduced under CCPL:
http://creativecommons.org/licenses/by/2.0/legalcode

Original advertisements from contemporary sources including *The
Knobkerrie* and *Diamond News*, 1871-1885

ISBN: 0-9553936-1-2
        978-0-9553936-1-7

" 'Feed the Beast' is the counsel given by Du Maurier's experienced wife to the young friend who asks her how a husband may be kept at home. This little volume shows how it may be done in an immense variety of ways; it supplies also a good store of useful information and hints upon every description of domestic matters."

Cape Times, 1889, on the first edition of the *Colonial Household Guide*, by Mrs A. R. Barnes.

CAPE GOVERNMENT RAILWAYS
(MIDLAND SYSTEM).

Tenders for Refreshment Room,
NAAUWPOORT STATION.

Tenders are invited for One Year's Leave as from the 1st August next, of the Refreshment Room at Naauwpoort Station.

Sealed Tenders to be sent to the Undersigned, from whom further information may be obtained, not later than Noon, on the 25th proximo, marked on the outside, "Tenders for Naauwpoort Refreshment Room."

The highest or any Tender not necessarily accepted.

A. W. HOWELL,
Traffic Manager.

1890 PREFACE.

THE chief object of this book is to assist in their duties the housewives and mothers of the colony. Such persons have been greatly puzzled at times in taking up a book of cookery written in England to find something suitable for preparation with colonial materials; for this reason many such recipes as are usually met with in a ponderous volume have been rejected, while their place has been filled by others more in favour in the colony, the greater part of which have been fairly tried and found to answer well.

Nothing contributes so much to the discomfort of a home as badly or wastefully cooked food, and it is hoped the book will assist those who have had little or no opportunity of learning to cook until they find themselves in a home of their own; who yet, being apt to learn, may only need a little practical guidance to enable them to succeed.

The latter part of the book, on general household subjects, etc., will, it is believed, prove helpful to those who require such assistance.

The Second Edition of this work contains a large amount of further useful and special information, and many new recipes have been added. For the benefit of our Dutch housewives, it is still intended, if the circulation of this edition be successful, to publish it at an early date in Dutch, and with this object it is hoped many will endeavour to make "The Colonial Household Guide " extensively known.

KIMBERLEY, SOUTH AFRICA.

2006 PREFACE.

Mrs Barnes' *Colonial Household Guide* was only the third or fourth English-language cookery book ever to be published in Africa: the first, a pamphlet printed in Pietermaritzburg, was produced just 15 years or so before Mrs Barnes' guide to domestic management was published in 1889.

To a modern reader perhaps the most striking aspect of Mrs Barnes' work is that it identifies a cuisine and lifestyle that, barely three generations after the 1820 settlers arrived in South Africa from the United Kingdom, was already in many aspects distinctly different from that of the British middle classes. Like her contemporaries Miss A. G. Hewitt and Hildegonda Duckitt, Mrs Barnes revels in the use of local ingredients and unfamiliar techniques: her Plum Pudding No. 2 recipe casually suggests substituting an ostrich egg for the 12 hen's eggs otherwise required!

Other recipes display a refreshing familiarity with ingredients that have not historically formed part of the traditional British African settler repertoire—the fruity sourness of tamarind pulp in a curry, or the aroma of wood-smoke lending savour to sweet, buttery kernels of mealies.

This is definitely the cuisine of acculturation: British colonists adopting ingredients and cooking techniques from the indigenous population as well as from earlier generations of European settlers and the Malay and Indian slaves they imported. Mrs Barnes even recommends a traditional medicinal plant (the "Goonah", or Sour Fig (*Carpobrotus edulis*)) of the Khokhoi people as a remedy for a sore throat, and gives precise and matter-of-fact instructions for preparing a traditional African cow-dung floor.

For this reprinted edition I have chosen not to include Mrs Barnes' section on South African gardening, and the extended essay on poultry-rearing by the appropriately-named Mr Chick. I have also tidied up some printing errors and idiosyncratic spelling choices—for example, caraway for carraway, and replaced brede with the more common bredie. Apart from that, the work is as Mrs Barnes wrote it. I need hardly add that many of the household hints, child-rearing advice and medical advice do not accord with modern practice, and should not be followed: they should be viewed as historical curiosities and are given for interest only.

LONDON, UNITED KINGDOM

FRESH FISH
EVERY DAY.

READY CLEANED FISH,
AT LOW PRICES,
14, DARLING STREET
(ADJOINING MASONIC HOTEL),

Large Stock of Salt Fish always on Hand.

CAPE FISH COMP.
A. W. AYLES, Manager.

CONTENTS.

Contents

Contents

Contents

Contents

11

Contents

Contents

Contents

Contents

Contents

Contents

Contents

Contents

Contents

Contents